THE PARABLES OF JESUS

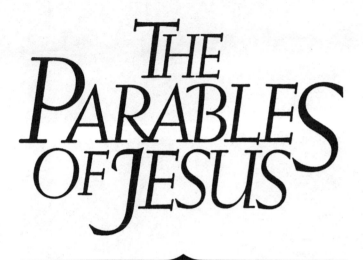

THE PARABLES OF JESUS

by

JAMES MONTGOMERY BOICE

MOODY PRESS
CHICAGO

© 1983 by
THE MOODY BIBLE INSTITUTE
OF CHICAGO

Library of Congress Cataloging in Publication Data

Boice, James Montgomery, 1932-
 The Parables of Jesus.

 1. Jesus Christ—Parables—Sermons. 2. Presbyterian Church—Sermons. 3. Sermons, American.
 I. Title.
 BT375.2.B56   1983   226'.806   82-18809
 ISBN: 0-8024-0163-5

4 5 Printing/GB/Year 87 86 85

Printed in the United States of America

TO HIM

who opened His mouth in parables
and uttered things hidden since
the creation of the world

CONTENTS

PARABLES OF THE CHRISTIAN LIFE

PARABLES OF JUDGMENT

PREFACE

When I began preaching on the parables of Jesus at Tenth Presbyterian Church in the winter of 1980-81, I had no intention of reducing the sermons to written form. In fact, the opposite was the case. I had gone through a difficult year at the church and was looking for a sermon series that could be prepared and preached without unusual amounts of extra work and could then be forgotten. Instead, I found myself enraptured by the parables and eager to treat them in as comprehensive a manner as possible.

I also found that others were being blessed by them. One young man had been sitting through the morning and evening services for years. He had a church background and had joined the church some time before, giving a credible profession of faith. But as he listened to the expositions he began to sense that, in spite of his profession of faith, all was not well with his soul. He knew the right doctrines and could say the right words, but there had been no real changes in his life. One Sunday evening, after the exposition of one of the parables of salvation, the wife of one of my assistants asked him if he had committed his life to the Lord Jesus Christ and if he really was born again. When he replied that he had not, and was not, she had the opportunity to lead him to personal faith.

That is what the parables of Jesus do, perhaps more than any comparable portion of Scripture. Other sections of the Bible give us grand theology. Some move us to grateful response to God. But the parables break through mere words and make us ask whether there has indeed been any real difference in our lives. Isn't that what we should expect, since the parables come from the lips of Jesus? No one was ever better than Jesus at getting through pretense to reality.

So far as I know, no one has grouped the parables precisely as I have done. I do not suggest that my arrangement is better, but as I worked with the Lord's stories it seemed to me that they lent themselves to a meaningful fivefold grouping: 1. parables of the kingdom, 2. parables of salvation, 3. parables of wisdom and folly, 4. parables of the Christian life, and 5. parables of judgment. Not surprisingly, those are also five natural groupings of our Lord's other teachings. It seemed to me, moreover, that some of the stories should most properly be treated together in one message rather than as separate studies. So, I have grouped three parables together in chapter 2 and two parables in chapter 3. Chapter 5 contains three parables that obviously are linked together. Chapters 15, 17, and 21 also contain a treatment of two parables each. After pulling the material together I discovered that each grouping contains at least one of the best-known and best-loved parables.

In the preface to each of my books I like to thank the congregation of Tenth Presbyterian Church, which kindly and unselfishly permits me to spend much of my time in sermon preparation and writing. That means less time for visiting and counseling, but they are happy with this arrangement in most cases. I also want to thank my secretary, Caecilie M. Foelster, who works with me in each stage of preparing the sermon material for publication. Without her speed and expertise I could not have produced the number of books I have been able to produce during the past fifteen years.

The dedication of this book is "to Him who opened His mouth in parables and uttered things hidden since the creation of the world." Those words come from Psalm 78:2 and are quoted in Matthew 13:35 as fulfilled by Jesus through His teaching in parables. Some of those hidden things became clear to me as I prepared these studies. I trust they will become so for others as they read these chapters.

PARABLES
OF THE
KINGDOM

1

THE SEED
AND THE SOIL

(Matthew 13:1-23)

That same day Jesus went out of the house and sat by the lake.
Such large crowds gathered around him that he got into a boat
and sat in it, while all the people stood on the shore. Then he
told them many things in parables, saying: "A farmer went out
to sow his seed. As he was scattering the seed, some fell along
the path, and the birds came and ate it up. Some fell on rocky
places, where it did not have much soil. It sprang up quickly,
because the soil was shallow. But when the sun came up, the
plants were scorched, and they withered because they had no
root. Other seed fell among thorns, which grew up and choked
the plants. Still other seed fell on good soil, where it produced a
crop—a hundred, sixty or thirty times what was sown. He who
has ears, let him hear."

One of my daughters has been singing a song about Jesus that
contains the line "Jesus was a story-tellin' man." When I first heard
that line it seemed a bit flip, as so many contemporary Christian
songs are. But as I thought about it I realized that it contains a real
truth: though Jesus was much more than a storyteller, He was at least
that, and as a result the people of His day flocked to Him and heard
Him gladly (Mark 12:37).

Christ's words were always picturesque. He spoke of camels creeping through the hole in a needle (Matt. 19:24), of people trying to remove specks from another's eye when a plank was in their own (Matt. 7:5). He referred to a house divided against itself, destined to fall down (Mark 3:25), to tossing children's bread to dogs (Mark 7:27). He warned against the "yeast" of the Pharisees (Mark 8:15). Strictly speaking, however, those are not stories. The stories Jesus told fall into a particular category of story known as *parable.* A parable is a story taken from real life (or a real-life situation) from which a moral or spiritual truth is drawn. Examples are many: the prodigal son (Luke 15:11-32), the good Samaritan (Luke 10:25-37), the Pharisee and the tax collector (Luke 18:9-14), the wedding banquet (Matt. 22:1-14; Luke 14:15-24), the sheep and the goats (Matt. 25:31-46), and others, including the parables of the kingdom that will occupy our attention in this first set of studies. By my count there are about twenty-seven parables, though some are closely related and may simply be different versions of the same story.

Parables differ from fables in that a fable is not a real situation. An example of a fable is any of Aesop's stories, in which animals talk. In those stories the animals are simply people in disguise. Parables also differ from allegories, since in an allegory each or nearly each detail has meaning. C. S. Lewis's *Chronicles of Narnia* are essentially allegories. In the parables of Jesus not every detail has meaning. Indeed, to try to force meaning into each one can produce strange and even demonstrably false doctrines. Parables are merely real-life stories from which one or possibly a few basic truths are drawn.

Parables of the Kingdom

If a person were to begin reading the New Testament at page one (Matt. 1:1) and read consecutively, he would read quite a while before encountering this important element of our Lord's teaching. In fact, he would have to read one-fourth of Matthew's gospel, chapters 1-12, before coming upon even the first of the parables. But with chapter 13 that suddenly changes—here, not one but *seven* parables are recorded. They have one theme, the kingdom of God, and so are called the "parables of the kingdom."

It is no accident that these are the first parables encountered. It is sometimes said that Matthew's gospel presents the Lord Jesus Christ as "king of Israel," just as Mark presents Him as the "Son of Man" and

Luke as the "servant." But whether we give Matthew that thematic emphasis or not, there is no doubt that Christ's proclamation of the kingdom is a major theme of Matthew's gospel. The very first verse introduces Jesus as "the son of David," Israel's great king. Jesus' forerunner, John the Baptist, is said to have come preaching "the kingdom of heaven" (Matt. 3:2). Jesus Himself made that the first theme of His itinerant ministry (Matt. 4:17). Some regard the Sermon on the Mount (Matt. 5-7) as the ethics of the kingdom; the miracles of chapters 8-12 demonstrate the kingdom's power. Since this is Matthew's early emphasis, we should not be surprised that the first parables develop this theme.

It is also no accident that the parables are presented in the order in which we have them, although methods of relating the seven stories differ. The most obvious division is into two sets of four and three respectively. In the first four (the sower and the seed, the enemy who sows tares, the mustard seed, and the yeast) Jesus speaks before the multitudes. The last three (the parables of the hidden treasure, the fine pearl, and the dragnet) are spoken before the disciples only. Some have grouped the parables by twos: (1) the parables involving planting and harvesting, (2) the parables of the mustard seed and the leaven, (3) parables that stress the kingdom's value—the treasure and the pearl, and (4) the parable of the dragnet.

Both of these classifications suggest a development, but I prefer a third system of classification. To my mind the first parable stands alone, since it deals with the origin of the kingdom. The next three belong together, since (as I hope to demonstrate) they picture Satan's desire to thwart the kingdom's growth. Parables five and six go together and show the attitude of those who vigorously seek the kingdom despite Satan's wiles. The last parable, the dragnet, shows the kingdom's consummation. Taken together the stories show the nature, origin, hindrances to, and victory of Christ's work of spreading His gospel through His messengers between the days of His first coming and His coming again.

THE PARABLE OF THE SOWER

The first parable is an ideal one with which to begin, since (obviously enough) it deals with the beginnings or origins of the kingdom. Here it is compared to a farmer sowing seed. "A farmer went out to sow his seed . . ." (Matt. 13:3-9). Not all of Christ's parables are explained. In fact, most are not. But this one is (vv. 18-23), and the explanation that Jesus gives is our starting point. The seed is the gospel of the kingdom, and the soil is the human heart (v. 19). The emphasis is on the various kinds of hearts and how they reject or receive Christ's message.

The first type of soil represents the *hard heart,* of which there are many today as well as in Christ's time. It is described as soil along the path (v. 4). Such ground has been trampled down by the many feet that have passed that way over scores of years. Because the soil is hard, the seed that falls there merely lies on the path and does not sink in, and the birds (which Christ compares to the devil or the devil's workers) soon snatch it away. What is it that makes the human heart hard? There can be only one answer: sin. Sin hardens the heart, and the heart that is hardened sins even more.

That type of person is described in the first chapter of Romans. He or she begins by suppressing the truth about God that may be known from nature (vv. 18-20), plunges inevitably into spiritual ignorance and moral degradation (vv. 21-31), and eventually comes not only to practice the sins of the heathen but to *approve* them as well (v. 32). Here we see both halves of the circle; sin leads to a rejection of God and God's truth, and the rejection of God's truth leads to even greater sin. What is it that leads such a person to reject the truth of God in the first place? According to Paul, it is a determined opposition to the nature of God Himself, which the apostle describes as human "godlessness and wickedness" (Rom. 1:18).

Virtually all of God's attributes—whether sovereignty, holiness, omniscience, immutability, or even the divine love—are offensive to the natural man, if properly understood. So rather than repent of sin and turn for mercy to a God who is altogether sovereign, holy, knowing, and unchangeable, men and women suppress what knowledge they have and refuse to seek out that additional knowledge that could be the salvation of their souls.

Recently I heard a conversation between two women in which one asked, "Why is America in such a declining moral state today?"

Her friend replied, "Because the people love sin." I cannot think of anything more profound than that. That is the message of Romans 1 in five words. *People love sin.* Sin hardens their hearts. Therefore, they will not receive the gospel of the kingdom of God when it is preached to them.

The opposition of the unregenerate heart to God's sovereignty is particularly evident in these kingdom parables, for kingdom means *rule*, and rule is the same as sovereignty. When Jesus came preaching the kingdom of God, He came preaching God's right to rule over the minds and hearts of all people. But that is precisely what the people involved did not want. Adam did not want it. He had great freedom, but he was offended by God's unreasonable and arbitrary (so he judged) restriction in the case of the tree of the knowledge of good and evil. If God exercised His sovereignty at that point, it was here that Adam would rebel. So he did—and fell, carrying the race with him. That spirit of rebellion against the sovereign God works itself out in history until eventually the Lord Jesus Christ Himself comes to earth and the response of His people is: "We will not have this man to rule over us."

So it is also today. That is probably the greatest reason for the rejection of the gospel of God's grace in Jesus Christ at this or any other time in history. I heard of a man who said, "I believe that Jesus is the Son of God and that He died for sinners. But I guess I just don't want to give Him my life. I want to make my own decisions."

The second type of soil stands for the *shallow heart*. Jesus described it as soil covering rocky ground. When the seed fell there it sank in, but only to a very shallow depth. It sprang up quickly, but it also faded quickly in the sun's heat because it had no root. Jesus later described that person: "What was sown on rocky places is the man who hears the word and at once receives it with joy. But since he has no root, he lasts only a short time. When trouble or persecution comes because of the word, he quickly falls away" (vv. 20-21).

Many people fit that description. We see them in our thriving evangelical churches. Their shallow hearts are attracted to the joy and excitement of a church where much is happening. They hear the gospel and seem to fit in. Many even make a profession of faith. But then some difficulty comes—loss of a job, misunderstandings with other Christians, sickness, even a bad romance—and just as suddenly as they once seemed to embrace the faith, they fall away, because they were really never born again.

Not long ago I noticed an extreme case. The newspapers reported the arrest in Lakeland, Florida of a man named Joseph Paul Franklin. He was wanted for questioning about a year-long series of shootings in Salt Lake City, Johnstown (Pennsylvania), Fort Wayne, Cincinnati,

Minneapolis, and Oklahoma City. He had grown up in a bad home, had dropped out of school at seventeen, and began getting into trouble, with several arrests for carrying concealed weapons and disorderly conduct. But then, as one magazine went on to say in tracing his early life, "he became an Evangelical Christian."[1] After that he became a Nazi and then a Ku Klux Klansman. At one point he told friends he was going to join Ian Smith's Rhodesian army.

I had been reading that news item with only minimal interest, but when I came to the line about his being an "Evangelical Christian" my attention picked up. I wondered why that had been slipped in and whether it was just one more attempt to discredit genuine Christianity. I do not think it was; Franklin had actually gone through Christianity as one stage in his warped development, and the magazine was simply reporting that fact fairly. The tragedy is not that such a thing is reported but that there are far too many in Franklin's category within our churches. Just being in church, mouthing the things you hear other people say, does not make you a Christian. Yours may be the shallow heart. Yours may be the rocky soil.

The third type of soil stands for the *strangled heart,* strangled by things. The Lord describes those things as thorns, and says, "What was sown among the thorns is the man who hears the word, but the worries of this life and the deceitfulness of wealth choke it, making it unfruitful" (v. 22). I do not need to point out how many lives are choked by riches today. It was true even in Jesus' day; we know that because of our Lord's many warnings against riches: "I tell you the truth, it is hard for a rich man to enter the kingdom of heaven" (Matt. 19:23); "It is easier for a camel to go through the eye of a needle than for a rich man to enter the kingdom of God" (Mark 10:25); "Woe to you who are rich, for you have already received your comfort" (Luke 6:24).

On one occasion a rich young man turned away from Jesus sorrowfully because Jesus had told him to sell everything he had and give it to the poor, and he was unwilling to do it (Luke 18:23). But if that was true in Jesus' day among people whom we would regard for the most part as very, very poor, how much truer it is in ours. How much more choked we are with riches—we who have cars and houses and boats and bank accounts and all the modern gadgets of our materialistic culture.

1. *Time,* 10 November 1980, p. 22.

There is this point, too: riches do not choke a person all at once. It is a gradual process. Like the weeds in Christ's parable, riches grow up gradually. Slowly, very slowly, they strangle the buddings of spiritual life within. Beware of that if you either have possessions or are on your merry way to acquiring them. Above all, beware if you are saying, "I need to provide for myself now. I'll think about spiritual things when I'm older." Jesus warned against that in another story about a man whose fields produced such a good crop that he tore down his barns and built bigger ones, saying to himself, "You have plenty of good things laid up for many years. Take life easy; eat, drink and be merry." Jesus' words were, "You fool! This very night your life will be demanded from you. Then who will get what you have prepared for yourself?" (Luke 12:16-21).

The last type of soil is the one to which the entire parable has been heading. It is the *open heart,* the heart that receives the gospel like good soil receives seed. This soil produces a good crop, "yielding a hundred, sixty or thirty times what was sown" (v. 23). Here many minor points might be made. We could show that only a portion (in the parable, one-fourth) of the preaching of the gospel bears fruit — in Christ's or any other age. We could show that the only sure evidence of a genuine reception of the Word of God in a person's life is the bringing forth of spiritual fruit. We could show that the presence of fruit is the important thing, not the amount (at least in most cases). But those points are less important than the main one: it is only the open heart that receives the benefit of the preaching of the gospel and is saved.

Is your heart an open heart? Are you receptive to God's truth? Do you allow it to settle down into your life and thinking so that it turns you from sin, directs your faith to Jesus, and produces the Holy Spirit's fruit? You may say, "I'm afraid not. I wish my heart was like that, but I'm afraid it is hard or shallow or strangled by this world's goods. What can I do?"

The answer is that you can do nothing, any more than soil can change its nature. But although you can do nothing, there is one who can — the divine Gardener. He can break up the hard ground, uproot the rocks, and remove the thorns. That is your hope — not you, but the Gardener. Notice what He says through the prophet Ezekiel, who wrote to the hard-hearted of his day. "I will sprinkle clean water on you, and you will be clean; I will cleanse you from all your impurities and from all your idols. I will give you a new heart and put a new spirit in you; I will remove from you your heart of stone and give you a heart of flesh. And I will put my Spirit in you and move you to follow my decrees and be careful to keep my laws" (Ezek. 36:25-27).

I think of that rich young man who turned away from Jesus sorrowfully. After Jesus had remarked how difficult it was for the rich to enter the kingdom of God, the disciples asked, "Who then can be saved?" They recognized the dimensions of the problem.

Jesus replied, "What is impossible with men is possible with God" (Luke 18:26-27). In other words, "With God all things are possible" (Matt. 19:26). And so they are! They are possible for *you*. Come to Christ and allow Him to give you a heart that will receive the gospel.

2

THE WORK OF
THE ENEMY

(Matthew 13:24-43)

Jesus told them another parable: "The kingdom of heaven is like a man who sowed good seed in his field. But while everyone was sleeping, his enemy came and sowed weeds among the wheat, and went away. When the wheat sprouted and formed heads, then the weeds also appeared.

"The owner's servants came to him and said, 'Sir, didn't you sow good seed in your field? Where then did the weeds come from?'

" 'An enemy did this,' he replied.

"The servants asked him, 'Do you want us to go and pull them up?'

" 'No,' he answered, 'because while you are pulling the weeds, you may root up the wheat with them. Let both grow together until the harvest. At that time I will tell the harvesters: First collect the weeds and tie them in bundles to be burned, then gather the wheat and bring it into my barn.' "

He told them another parable: "The kingdom of heaven is like a mustard seed, which a man took and planted in his field. Though it is the smallest of all your seeds, yet when it grows, it is the largest of garden plants and becomes a tree, so that the birds of the air come and perch in its branches."

He told them still another parable: "The kingdom of heaven is like yeast that a woman took and mixed into a large amount of flour until it worked all through the dough."

Nothing good has ever come into the world without opposition, and that is especially true in spiritual matters. Here we face not only the hostility and opposition of mere people like ourselves, but satanic or demonic opposition as well. That is why the Bible wants us to be on our guard against the devil who, we are told, "prowls around like a roaring lion looking for someone to devour" (1 Pet. 5:8). The Scripture alerts us to the devil's "schemes." He must not be able to outwit us (2 Cor. 2:11).

Since we have an enemy who is so fiercely opposed to the extension of God's rule on earth, we should not be surprised to find the Lord warning us against his devices in the parables of the kingdom in Matthew 13. Jesus does this quite clearly in the second parable, showing how the devil, like an enemy of a certain farmer, sows weeds in God's field—that is, scatters his unbelievers among God's believers. Jesus also does this in the third and fourth parables, in my judgment, though He speaks there without explanation. He tells of a mustard seed that grew up to be a great tree and of yeast that a woman mixed into a large amount of dough. These parables alert us to strategies Satan has been using to hinder the work of God in this seed-sowing age between the time of Christ's first coming and His coming again.

PARABLE OF THE WEEDS

The first of these parables is the easiest to interpret (though it does have some difficult parts), both because much of it is self-evident, and because the Lord explains it. The details of the parable itself are given in verses 24-30 of Matthew 13.

In discussing this passage some have made much of a detail in Christ's explanation, found in verse 38. In the previous verse Jesus had explained that "the one who sowed the good seed is the Son of Man"—an explanation that no doubt applies to the first parable as well and shows that all the parables are somewhat linked. Then He goes on to say, "The field is the world" (v. 38). Some have stressed that point, arguing that if the field is the world, it cannot be the church. Therefore, Christ's prohibition against trying to separate the weeds from the grain before the final judgment does *not* apply to church discipline. So the church, in spite of Christ's warning, should try to be as pure as possible.

The concern that leads to that interpretation is a valid one, namely, that the church should strive to maintain purity. Other passages in the New Testament call upon us to work for that goal. But to argue for that idea gets the interpretation of the parable off track. For one thing, it is impossible here to make a rigid distinction between the world and the church, because a little further on Jesus speaks of the angels weeding out of *His kingdom* everything that causes sin and all who do evil (v. 41, emphasis added). God's kingdom is not the world in general, so any interpretation that builds exclusively on the phrase "the field is the world" is suspect.

Again, what is the point of the devil's planting children "in the world" in a general way, if all it means is that the devil's children and God's children live side by side? At best that is self-evident. Besides, if that is what Jesus means, the parable is not even stating the situation in the best way. If the field is the world apart from the church, it would be more correct to say that the devil's children are in the world already and that it is Jesus, rather than Satan, who plants His seed among the seed that is already growing. It would be Jesus who does the new thing, not Satan. He is planting seed that is to grow up into spiritual fruit in the lives of His people. But as Jesus tells the story, He stresses what *Satan* is doing, and that must be after Jesus has already sown His seed. The devil is mixing counterfeit Christians in among true Christians to hinder God's work.

So that is the real message. Whether the field is the world or the church is actually irrelevant. The point is simply that the devil is going to bring forward people (whether in the church or out of it) so much like true Christians, yet not Christians, that even the servants of God will not be able to tell them apart. Consequently, although we want a pure church and will certainly exercise church discipline to the best of our ability in clear cases, we must not think that we will achieve our full desire in this age. Even in our exercise of valid church discipline we must be extremely careful not to discourage or damage some for whom Christ died.

I find the following applications of this parable.

1. *If the devil is mixing his people in among true Christians, then we should be alert to that fact.* We should be on our guard not to be

taken in, and we should not be surprised if the devil's people show up in strange places or eventually show their true colors by abandoning Christianity entirely. In 2 Corinthians Paul gives just such a warning, pointing out that "Satan himself masquerades as an angel of light" and that "it is not surprising, then, if his servants masquerade as servants of righteousness" (2 Cor. 11:14-15). "Servants of righteousness" means "ministers." Thus the old proverb, "When you look for the devil don't forget to look in the pulpit." Again, we are not to be surprised if some like this eventually repudiate the faith and leave Christian fellowship. John also wrote of such, saying, "They went out from us, but they did not really belong to us. For if they had belonged to us, they would have remained with us; but their going showed that none of them belonged to us" (1 John 2:19).

2. *The mixed nature of the Christian assembly should not be an excuse for unbelievers to refuse to come to Christ.* Jesus did not pretend (nor should we) that the Christian church is perfect. Sometimes unbelievers say, "I'm not a Christian because the church is filled with hypocrites." But that is itself a hypocritical statement. It implies that the one making it is better than those whom he rejects. At best it is not the whole truth—there are deeper reasons why people will not become Christians. But the real problem is that if the objection were to be met (that is, if hypocrisy and other sins were to be eliminated entirely among the people of God), then there would be no place for the objector! He or she would not fit in. There is a place for him or her only because Jesus came "not . . . to call the righteous, but sinners" to repentance (Matt. 9:13).

3. *No one should take comfort in sin.* The church is impure; we cannot always distinguish between the wheat and tares in this age. But a day is coming when that distinction will be made. The harvest will come. The wheat will be gathered into God's barn, and the tares will be burned. As a result, we should examine ourselves as to whether we are true children of God or not. And we should be careful to make our "calling and election sure," as Peter indicates (2 Pet. 1:10).

THE MUSTARD SEED AND YEAST

The next two of Christ's parables (vv. 31-33) belong together. Each should help us to understand the other, but of all the parables Christ told, none has produced such diametrically opposed interpretations as these two. What are those diverse interpretations? On the one hand, some teachers see these as parables of the kingdom's expansion and growth, so that in time it actually comes to fill the whole world. An example is William M. Taylor, who has left us an excellent book on the parables. He writes of the story of the mustard seed:

> *A great result from a small beginning,* a large growth from a little germ—that is the one thought of the parable, and of that the Lord declares that the kingdom of heaven upon the earth is an instance.

He writes of the yeast,

> The great truth here illustrated, then, is that the Lord Jesus Christ, by his coming and work, introduced into humanity an element which works a change on it, that shall continue to operate until the whole is transformed—therein resembling leaven, hidden by a woman in three measures of meal until the whole was leavened.[1]

Most postmillennialists and many amillennialists take this view since it fits their eschatology to have a parable that tells of the kingdom's triumph in the world before Christ's return.

The other viewpoint is represented by a man like Arno C. Gaebelein, who sees the parables as teaching an abnormal and harmful bureaucratic expansion of the church and the devil's work of undermining it by the infusion of sin, represented by the yeast. He writes, "All these parables show the growth of *evil,* and are prophecies extending over the entire age in which we live."[2]

What are normal people to think about these two interpretations?

We should say first that, whatever our interpretation of the parables might be, there is nevertheless much more theological agreement between people who take these two sides than the interpretations themselves would indicate. To be sure, there is a profound disagreement as to whether the kingdom of God is going to be

---

1. William M. Taylor, *The Parables of Our Saviour Expounded and Illustrated* (New York: A. C. Armstrong and Son, 1900), pp. 55, 60-61.
2. Arno C. Gaebelein, *The Gospel of Matthew: An Exposition* (New York: Loizeaux, 1910), p. 292.

victorious in this age. Postmillennialists would say yes. Premillennialists would say no. But even here there is a measure of agreement. Both acknowledge that Christians are sent out into the whole world with the gospel—the essence of the Great Commission. Both would agree that there has certainly been an effective and striking growth of Christianity from its small beginnings at the time of Christ's death to its position as a dominant world religion today.

Again, to look at the parable of the yeast, each side would acknowledge that the devil has certainly been effective in working evil into the visible church, greatly harming its effectiveness. So we may begin by realizing that—with the sole exception of whether the church is to be victorious in the world or only affect a part of it—*most* of the points any one interpreter would insist on would be accepted by the other side.

But we do have to think of the stories one way or the other. Since I have already indicated that I lump them together with the parable that tells of the devil's work, let me give my reasons for seeing them as I do.

First, the growth of a mustard seed into a tree is abnormal. That is, a mustard seed does not grow into a tree; it grows into a shrub. Anyone to whom Christ spoke would know that. So when He spoke of the great and unusual growth of this seed, His hearers would immediately have been alerted to the fact that something was wrong. If Jesus had wanted to stress the "victorious church" view, He should have referred to an acorn growing up to be an oak or a cedar seed growing up to be one of the mighty trees of Lebanon.

Second, in the context of Matthew 13 the birds, who (in this parable) rest in the mustard tree's branches (v. 32), have already (in parable one) been identified as the devil or the devil's messengers (v.19). It is true that an element of one parable need not necessarily carry the same meaning if it is used in the next, but it surely would be strange if an element that symbolized such evil at the start of the chapter carried a totally different meaning just thirteen verses later. Who are the birds who roost in the church's branches if not those whom the devil has sown among the organized church? If they are not Satan's people, then who they are is left unexplained. On the other hand, if the birds are the devil's followers, then there is an immediate and obvious carry-over into the parable of the yeast, for the yeast would represent the same thing as the birds do in verse 32.

The parable of the yeast would just add the thought that the presence of evil is pervasive.

Third, in nearly all cases in the Old Testament (and in Jewish life today) yeast is a symbol of evil. In the sacrificial laws of Israel it was excluded from every offering to the Lord made by fire. At the time of the feast of unleavened bread, every faithful Jew was to search his home for any trace of yeast and then get rid of it. That is done today by orthodox Jews and symbolizes for them, as it did earlier, the putting away of sin. Jesus spoke of the leaven (or yeast) of the Pharisees and Sadducees, and Herod, in each case meaning their evil influence (Matt. 16:12; Mark 8:15). Paul described deviation from the truth of the gospel as Satan's persuasion, adding that believers should beware since "a little yeast works through the whole batch of dough" (Gal. 5:9; cf. 1 Cor. 5:6). Some have argued that yeast is not always a symbol of evil, and that is true. Sometimes it is simply yeast. But when it has a symbolic meaning it is nearly always used of something evil rather than something good. It is difficult to see how an important and thoroughly understood symbol of evil could be used by Jesus to represent the exact opposite, namely, the blessed impact of His gospel on the world.

Finally, it is significant that these two parables are bracketed by that of the devil's work in sowing tares among the wheat (vv. 24-30), and Christ's explanation of that parable (vv. 36-43). This structure suggests they should be taken not as teaching something entirely different from the parable of the tares, but as expanding it.

THE SECULAR CHURCH

As Christians, we must be on guard against Satan's tactics. We are warned not only against his infusion of his own people into the Christian community, but also against the visible church's bureaucratic growth (which confuses size and structure with spiritual fruit) and against the infusion of evil into the lives even of believing people (which confuses a loving and forgiving spirit with treason to Christ's cause). In other words, we are to beware of the secular church and evangelical secularism as well.

The secular church is one dominated by the world, as much of the contemporary church is. It is characterized by the world's wisdom, the world's theology, the world's agenda, and the world's methods.

The evangelical church, when it is secular, is one that seeks to do God's work but in the world's way. It looks to the media and money rather than to God and His power, which is unleashed through prayer.

What can the evangelical church do if it finds that it has been permeated by the "yeast" of Satan's strategies? Under normal circumstances, yeast that has begun to work cannot be eradicated. That is why it is such a good picture of the evil that will be in the church and world until the return of the Lord Jesus Christ. But although in baking we would have little success in ridding dough of leaven, in the spiritual realm we can have successes—at least where we ourselves (and perhaps our immediate families and churches) are concerned. Paul writes to the Corinthians, "Get rid of the old yeast that you may be a new batch without yeast" (1 Cor. 5:7). In Galatians, where he has been talking about the yeast of legalism, he says, "It is for freedom that Christ has set us free. Stand firm, then, and do not let yourselves be burdened again by a yoke of slavery" (Gal. 5:1).

Satan is active. The yeast of the Pharisees will work. But "thanks be to God! He gives us the victory through our Lord Jesus Christ" (1 Cor. 15:57). In the next parables we are going to see the divinely imparted character of those who seize the kingdom and achieve that victory.

3

PEOPLE OF THE KINGDOM

(Matthew 13:44-46)

"The kingdom of heaven is like treasure hidden in a field. When a man found it, he hid it again, and then in his joy went and sold all he had and bought that field.

"Again, the kingdom of heaven is like a merchant looking for fine pearls. When he found one of great value, he went away and sold everything he had and bought it."

There is a caricature of Calvinism that takes issue with the doctrines of election and "irresistible" grace. It imagines a case in which a certain individual—we'll call him George—does not want to be saved. George loves sin, and never looks beyond it. Although he has heard the gospel of salvation by grace through faith in Jesus Christ, he has no interest in it personally. But God has elected this person. So, although George does not want to be saved, he is nevertheless dragged by the scruff of his neck into heaven "kicking and screaming," a most reluctant convert.

On the other hand, there is a second individual—let's call her Mary—who wants to be saved. Every time she hears the gospel she is enraptured by it. Whenever an invitation is given she is the first one out of her seat. But God has not elected her. Although she wants to be saved, she cannot be. God says, "Mary, this salvation of

Mine through Christ is not for you. You must remain where you are. You cannot come to heaven."

As I say, that is a misunderstanding of Calvinism, for in election and "irresistible" grace God does not disregard or act contrary to the will of any man or woman, as implied above. Rather, He regenerates the individual, as the result of which a will is born that now desires what the old will previously despised. Before, George hated Christ. Now he loves Him and so comes willingly when the gospel is preached. Again, if Mary desires to come, it is not in spite of God's predetermination in her case but because of it.

One commentator says, "When [people are] made over again . . . they come running irresistibly because they would not have it any other way. You can put all kinds of obstacles in their path, but they are men of violence. They are going to take the kingdom by force! When they find this pearl they are going to sell everything they have and get it. That hidden treasure is going to be theirs. They are going to thump on that door until it is opened. They are going to have because they hunger and thirst after righteousness."[1]

THE TREASURE AND THE PEARL

I have begun this way because the prior work of God in a person's heart is the underlying presupposition of the parables of the treasure and the pearl to which we now come. Those parables describe the kind of people who have already been made alive in Christ. To use the imagery of the first two parables, they are the ones in whom the seed of the gospel has already been planted and is beginning to bear fruit. In the first, a man finds a treasure in a field. Jesus says, "When [he] found it, he hid it again, and then in his joy went and sold all he had and bought that field." In the second, He describes a merchant looking for pearls. "When he found one of great value, he went away and sold everything he had and bought it" (vv. 44, 46).

The point of these parables lies in the nature and actions of those who discover the great treasure, which is the gospel. In this, the man who discovered the treasure and the merchant who found the pearl are identical. There is a point of contrast that should not be

---

1. John H. Gerstner, "The Atonement and the Purpose of God," in James M. Boice, ed., *Our Savior God: Addresses Presented to the Philadelphia Conference on Reformed Theology, 1977-1979* (Grand Rapids: Baker, 1980), p. 115.

overlooked, however. The man who found the hidden treasure was apparently not looking for it—his discovery was an accident—but in the case of the merchant, the finding of the pearl was the result of a long and faithful quest.

That contrast aptly describes the past experiences of people who find salvation. Some were not particularly anxious to find Christ— in fact, not even very interested in religion. They were going on their way when suddenly an unexpected thing confronted them: the gospel. They had never really seen it before. They were not seeking it. But there it was; and at once, with that insight granted by God's internal work of regeneration, they saw that this was a prize of far greater value than anything that had ever come into their lives previously. They saw themselves as sinners in need of a Savior. They saw Jesus as that Savior. They recognized that if they had Him, they had all else besides. So they turned to Him and believed, on the spot. Their case is an illustration of Isaiah's words, "I revealed myself to those who did not ask for me; I was found by those who did not seek me" (Isa. 65:1).

Perhaps you are like that, even as you read these words. You have not been seeking God. You have been reading merely to fill an idle moment, not to find salvation. But suddenly the way is open before you. Christ is present, and you are drawn to Him. If so, God is at work; be glad for that. Now follow through, as did the man who found the hidden treasure.

The other type of person is quite different. He is one who really had sought God and had found the way long and difficult. It is true that this person sought only because God had first come seeking him. It could be said of him as it is said in the hymn:

> I sought the Lord, and afterward I knew
> He moved my soul to seek him, seeking me;
> It was not I that found, O Savior true;
> No, I was found of thee.

But this person did not know that during his years of seeking. Those were dark years of false leads and harmful misunderstandings. At times he nearly despaired, but then the search was rewarded. The pearl of great price was before him, and now everything else was laid aside to secure that most valued object. Those are the ones of whom Jesus spoke when He said, "Ask and it will be given to you;

seek and you will find; knock and the door will be opened to you" (Matt. 7:7).

Perhaps you are that kind of person. You have not been indifferent to spiritual things but you have been seeking, and now the end of your quest is before you. Here is Jesus. Now you must believe on Him unto salvation. You have asked, and the answer has been given. You have sought, and Jesus is presented. Now you must knock and enter in by the opened door. Jesus said, "I am the gate; whoever enters through me will be saved" (John 10:9).

PURSUING THE PRIZE

Here is where the main lessons of the two parables are to be found, for although the man and the merchant were different up to the point at which the gospel treasure was before them, from then on their thoughts and actions were identical. What did they do? First, they recognized the value of what they had found. Second, they determined to have it. Third, they sold everything in order to make their purchase. Fourth, they acquired the treasure.

It is not surprising that the merchant recognized the value of that special pearl, for he had been seeking pearls and had presumably learned their value (or lack of value) through his seeking. Nor is it surprising that the man who discovered the hidden treasure saw its value. He was not seeking, but we can hardly imagine him casually kicking at the treasure with his foot and walking on. A treasure *is* valuable, after all. We are inclined to say that a person who discovers treasure anywhere or in any form and then walks away from it is a fool. But many do that with the gospel. The gospel is preached; it is shown to be the answer to our individual and community needs, for this life and for eternity. Despite that fact, millions simply walk away and continue in their spiritual poverty.

Do you want to know the character of one who has been made alive by God? He says with David, "I would rather be a doorkeeper in the house of my God than dwell in the tents of the wicked" (Ps. 84:10). He says of God's laws, "They are more precious than gold, than much pure gold" (Ps. 19:10). He declares, "Because I love your commands more than gold, more than pure gold, and because I consider all your precepts right, I hate every wrong path" (Ps. 119:127-28). He cries, "Forgetting what is behind and straining toward what is ahead, I press on toward the goal to win the prize for which God has called me heavenward in Christ Jesus" (Phil. 3:13-14). A person like that has already had a change of values. He has recognized the poverty of all that comes from men and women and has seen the true splendor of the gospel.

The second thing that characterized both the man who found the treasure and the merchant who discovered the pearl was their determination to have them once they had been discovered. The stories do not spell it out, but imagine the contrast. A person sees the value of his discovery but decides, as he reflects on it, that it would be too much trouble to acquire the treasure or the pearl for himself. He would have to adjust his priorities. He would have to sell his goods, change his life-style. That would take time and effort. It might be misunderstood by his family or friends. True, it would make him a rich man, but it would be too much trouble. We may imagine a situation like that, but such is not the case of the ones described in those parables.

May I interject a parenthesis at this point? The parable does not speak about those who owned the field and pearl originally. We are not told anything of their attitudes. But it is clear that they were willing to sell. God does not sell His favors, of course. The stories are not teaching that. But the point is, if you are *determined* to have what by the grace of God you perceive to be of inestimable value, then you may be sure that God is more than willing for you to have it. You may have it now. The price is only that you be willing to come to God in God's way. You must forget your own righteousness. You must be willing to trust in Christ alone. If you will come that way, turning from your sin to Jesus, then the treasure is yours. Christ has become your portion. God does not need to be persuaded. You are the one who needs persuasion. So wait no longer; believe today.

That brings us to the third point of similarity between the two individuals. Having recognized the value of their find and having determined to have it, they next sold all they had to make the purchase. I have already said that nothing in the stories is to be construed as teaching that salvation can be bought, except in the sense of Isaiah 55:1. "Come, all you who are thirsty, come to the waters; and you who have no money, come, buy and eat! Come, buy wine and milk without money and without cost." What, then, is the point of the man and the merchant selling their goods? Clearly, it is a picture of renouncing everything that might be a hindrance to attaining that great prize. Martin Luther's hymn has it right: "Let goods and kindred go, this mortal life also." Luther did not think for a moment that salvation could be purchased by the renunciation of those or any other valued possessions, but he was determined that nothing, not even life itself, should keep him from God's kingdom.

Charles H. Spurgeon had a sermon on the merchant and the pearl entitled "A Great Bargain," in which he suggested a number of things we must sell off in order to have Jesus. The first is old prejudices. All of us have some ideas of what it means to please God, but before God regenerates us those are inevitably wrong, if for no other reason than that "the man without the Spirit does not accept the things that come from the Spirit of God, for they are foolishness to him, and he cannot understand them, because they are spiritually discerned" (1 Cor. 2:14). The unregenerate person thinks of God as a man and, if the truth be told, of himself as almost a god. He thinks of earning his way. He thinks that God must take note of his good deeds and that, if God does not, he wants no part of Him. He thinks he would rather be in hell with nice people like himself than in heaven with those religious folks he finds so offensive. All this goes when one finds Christ. Old prejudices die. Old values are overturned. The errors of past thinking are sold off.

Again, the person who would have Christ must dispose of his or her self-righteousness.

It will not fetch much, but I daresay you think it is a fine thing. Hitherto you have been very good, and your own esteem of yourself is that as touching the commandments—"all these have I kept from my youth up." And what with a good deal of church going, or attendance at the meeting house, and a few extra prayers on a Christmas day and on Good Friday, and just a little dose of sacraments, you feel yourself in tolerable good case. Now, my friend, that old moth-eaten righteousness of yours that you are so proud of you must sell off and get rid of it, for no man can be saved by the righteousness of Christ while he puts any trust in his own. Sell it all off, every rag of it. And suppose nobody will buy it, at any rate you must part with it. Assuredly it is not worth putting amongst the filthiest of rags, for it is worse than they are.[2]

Yet how we value our own righteousness! We want it to be esteemed by others. It is hard for us to say that we are miserable sinners in need of a salvation that comes entirely by grace. But that is what we must say. Self-righteousness must go. Will you not sell yours off? What am I bid for it? The bid is enough! Let us sell it now. Be done with it, and come to Jesus.

Finally, you must sell off your sinful pleasures and practices, too. It is not pleasure itself that must be sold off. There are holy pleasures, for the saints are a joyful people. It is only sinful pleasure that must go, for you cannot serve God and sin. You cannot say that you love Christ and fail to keep His commandments.

Do you find that hard? Do you draw back? Is that too great a price to pay for salvation? If so, you are not the man of Christ's parable who finds the treasure and sells all he has to have it. You are not the merchant who trades off everything to possess the great pearl. You have not even properly seen the value of what you are rejecting.

Draw back, then! Reject the Lord Jesus Christ! He does not display His treasures for those who do not want them. Go your own way! Cling to your prejudices, your self-righteousness, your sinful pleasures! There are plenty of others who want Christ, and they will come. Heaven will not be empty. The banquet table will be filled with guests.

But God forbid that that should be so in your case! Rather let it be said of you as it was said by the author of Hebrews: "We are not of those who shrink back and are destroyed, but of those who believe and are saved" (Heb. 10:39).

Having recognized the value of their discovery and having sold everything in their desire to have it, the man who discovered the treasure and the merchant who discovered the pearl then made their purchase. They acquired that on which their desires had been set.

That purchase speaks of individual appropriation. It tells us that salvation does not consist merely in seeing the value of Christ's work and wanting it for oneself. It stresses that Christ must actually

---

2. Charles Haddon Spurgeon, "A Great Bargain," in *Metropolitan Tabernacle Pulpit*, vols. 7-63 (Pasadena, Tex.: Pilgrim Publications, 1972), 24:403.

become ours by faith, which is the means of appropriation. Faith has three elements. There is an intellectual element, in which we recognize the truths of the gospel. There is an emotional (heart) element, in which we find ourselves being drawn to what we recognize. There is also a volitional element, in which we actually make a commitment to Him whom the gospel reveals. That means that salvation is an individual matter. People are not saved by Jesus in groups. They are saved one by one as by the grace of God they recognize their need and come to Jesus in simple faith that He is who He claimed to be (the Son of God) and that He did what He claimed He would do (provide for our salvation through His death on our behalf). The man in the field did not allow someone else to buy the treasure in hopes that he might share in it. The merchant did not form a cooperative to acquire the pearl of great price. Each made the purchase individually.

You must not think, if you are teetering on the brink, that having renounced everything else for Jesus you will one day find yourself disappointed at what will have proved to be a bad bargain. You will not find yourself coming back with your treasure or pearl, hoping to get your property back. It is never that way. In the exchange described by these parables the men who made the purchase received a bargain. They make the deal of their lives, their fortune. From now on they will be the happiest of men.

So it will be for you. You are not called to poverty in Christ but to the greatest of spiritual wealth. You are not called to disappointment but to fulfillment. You are not called to sorrow but to joy. How could it be otherwise when the treasure is the only Son of God? How can the outcome be bad when it means salvation?

4

GOD'S KINGDOM CONSUMMATED

(Matthew 13:47-52)

"Once again, the kingdom of heaven is like a net that was let down into the lake and caught all kinds of fish. When it was full, the fishermen pulled it up on the shore. Then they sat down and collected the good fish in baskets, but threw the bad away. This is how it will be at the end of the age. The angels will come and separate the wicked from the righteous and throw them into the fiery furnace, where there will be weeping and gnashing of teeth."

"Have you understood all these things?" Jesus asked.

"Yes," they replied.

He said to them, "Therefore every teacher of the law who has been instructed about the kingdom of heaven is like the owner of a house who brings out of his storeroom new treasures as well as old."

In the second century before Christ the great rival to Roman power in the Mediterranean world was Carthage, the Phoenician city-state located on the north African coast. It had been founded in 822 B.C. and had become so powerful that for years it threatened the supremacy of Rome. What was to be done about Carthage? One Roman senator, Marcus Porcius Cato the elder, thought he knew— Carthage should be overthrown. From the time he arrived at that conclusion, it is said that he never made a speech before the Roman Senate on any topic that did not end with the warning: *Carthago delenda est* ("Carthage must be destroyed"). At last the warnings got through, and as the outcome of the third Punic War, Carthage was annihilated.

Cato's technique in dealing with the threat of Carthage is not the only time in history a point has been won by repetition. We think of Hitler repeating his lies against the Jews until seemingly the whole of Germany believed them; or, in quite a different way, of Winston Churchill telling the boys at the public school where he had been educated, "Never give up! Never give up! Never, never, never give up!"

The Lord Jesus Christ used repetition, too, and nowhere is it more evident than in the parables of the kingdom recorded in Matthew 13. There are very few points in any one of those parables that are not repeated in some form in at least one of the others. One point is that the work of the kingdom, begun by Jesus, is like sowing seed in a field. That is taught in the first parable on the different kinds of soil, and is repeated in the second, which tells of the devil's work in sowing tares among the wheat. The work of the devil is likewise repeated, if our understanding of the fourth and fifth parables is correct. He hinders God's work by sowing bad seed (parable two), encouraging an unnatural and secular church growth (parable three), and causing even the lives of true believers to be weakened by sin (parable four). Parables five and six, those of the hidden treasure and the valuable pearl, teach that the people of the kingdom are so changed by God that they perceive the value of salvation through Jesus Christ and give everything they have to obtain it.

THE DRAGNET

When we come to the last of the parables we find more repetition. Jesus introduces a new imagery (fishing), but the parable makes essentially the same points as parable two. The earlier parable told of wheat and tares growing up together until the time of the harvest. Then there is a gathering in of both followed by a separation. The wheat is gathered into the owner's barns; the tares are burned. In this, the last of the parables, there is also a gathering in of many kinds of fish followed by a separation of the good fish from the bad. In both parables Jesus describes a separation of the wicked from the righteous. We see the work of the angels. We even have a repetition of key phrases from Christ's explanation of the second parable: "the end of the age" (vv. 40, 49), and "throw them into the fiery furnace, where there will be weeping and gnashing of teeth" (vv. 42, 50).

But now we have a problem. What does the seventh parable teach that has not already been taught by the second? That is, why (in view of the earlier parable) is this one included? It is true, as we have indicated, that the others also involve repetition. But each, nevertheless, adds something new. The first two speak of sowing, but the first focuses on the kind of soil into which the seed falls, whereas the second focuses on the devil's work in sowing harmful seed. Similarly, the devil is described as active in parables two, three, and four, but in each case he is doing something different. Is there anything new in this last parable? Is there anything we would lose if it were not included?

The only element that might possibly be conceived of as new is the image of fishing, and it is tempting to think here of how Christ called fishermen to be His disciples: "Come, follow me, and I will make you fishers of men" (Matt. 4:19). We would like to think that the new element is our role in drawing men and women into the gospel net. But that is not the way Jesus interprets the parable. He compares the fishermen to angels, not to His earthly messengers. And the setting is not the time in which the church carries the gospel throughout the world, but the final judgment.

So what is new about the seventh parable? The mixture of fish in the gospel net? That is in the parable of the wheat and the tares. The angels' work? The separation? The terrible end of the wicked? Those elements are in the earlier parable as well.

As we make the comparisons, there is a point at which the repetition itself becomes the "new" thing, and the unique emphasis of the parable begins to be seen not only in what is repeated but in what is left out. Think of the elements of the other parables that are *not* present. There is no explanation of how the fish got into the water in the first place. There is no emphasis upon their growth or lack of it. There are no human workers, not even a devil. The only thing we have is the separation of the good fish from the bad, the wicked from the righteous, and the suffering of those who are cast into the fiery furnace. Therefore, I believe that the "new" element is the warning to the wicked. Their fate has already been described, but it was mixed in with other elements. Here it stands out for the simple reason that it is conspicuously alone.

It is as though Jesus is saying with all possible emphasis: *"There is a coming judgment, a separation, and the fate of the ungodly will be terrible in that day."*

A FINAL SEPARATION

Jesus' picture of the final judgment as a separation of good from bad fish (or a separation of wheat from tares) hits upon the essential nature of judgment, for the word "judgment" means to separate. In Hebrew, as in English, judgment refers chiefly to the work of a judge or lawgiver. But one meaning of the Hebrew word is "to discriminate" or make distinctions, and in Greek "judgment" *(krisis)* literally means "to divide." A crisis is something that confronts you with a choice; you must respond by going in one direction or another.

Jesus talked about judgment in that way. In later parables there is a separation between the five wise and five foolish virgins, the faithful and unfaithful servants, the sheep and the goats. In the parable of the rich man and Lazarus the point is made explicitly: "Between us and you a great chasm has been fixed, so that those who want to go from here to you cannot, nor can anyone cross over from there to us" (Luke 16:26).

There are three important facts about that separation. First, it is *absolute.* That is, in the day of God's judgment the time for mixture in any form will be over. Now we have mixture all the time. We do some good things, but our good is always mixed with evil. We have the redeemed people in the church, but we also have those who are the devil's children. However, when the Lord sends His angels to execute judgment those days will be over, and human beings will find themselves in one camp or the other. Either they will be with the blessed in heaven, having been cleansed from all sin by the redeeming work of Christ, or they will be in hell without Christ and without hope. No one will be partially in one camp and partially in the other.

The second fact about that separation is that it is *previously determined* in the sense that the grounds of the distinction will already have been laid on earth. What are they? Going back to Christ's earlier parables, it is a question of whether one has received the good seed of the gospel, whether one has believed in Christ. It is whether one has laid all else aside to gain the hidden treasure or purchase the valuable pearl. You know whether or not you have done that. In which camp are you? If you are not in Christ now, you will be without Him then. If you are with Him now, you will be with Him in the day of judgment.

Third, the separation is *permanent*. Nothing could be more permanent than the collecting of the good fish and the discarding of the bad. Nothing could be more permanent than the throwing of the tares into the fire to be burned. In that day the opportunity for repentance will be over. The day of salvation will be past.

I wish I could say that the reality will be different. But I cannot, for Jesus Himself does not. There is only one person who will tell you that. He is the devil, and he has been spreading that lie for centuries. He has told millions that the day of reckoning is always far off and that there will always be time for repentance or religion or whatever at a later date. In that way he has lulled millions to sleep, and they now drift on, oblivious to their danger. They are like the man who fell asleep in his car in the garage while the motor was running. The fumes of death were about him, but he was unaware of it. He was asleep and perished.

Do not listen to the devil's lies. He cares nothing for you. He is a condemned and evil being who, knowing that he must perish, takes his sole delight in drawing others after him to a common doom. Instead, listen to the Lord Jesus Christ, who speaks truth. He speaks it in this parable so you might know that judgment is real, separation is coming, and the time for repentance is now. Hear him! Believe him! Turn from anything that would keep you from Jesus and throw yourself upon Him and His work only.

GNASHING OF TEETH

The second point of Jesus' parable is the terrible fate of the unrighteous. I am glad Jesus taught that, and that it is not left for His ministers to imagine what the unbelievers' fate might be. How could we say that their end will be so bad that it can only be adequately compared to an eternal burning? How could we say that it will produce an eternal "weeping and gnashing of teeth"? No mere human being would dare predict that fate for another human being. Yet that is what Jesus does. He has more to say about hell than does any other person in the Bible.

What is it that makes hell so terrible, according to Jesus Christ? There are a number of elements, the first being *suffering*. That point is made in the parable of the dragnet, for having described how the wicked are thrown into the fiery furnace, Jesus then pictures them as "weeping and gnashing" their teeth. Often someone will ask me whether hell has literal fire. That is the imagery the Bible uses for hell, but I know the Bible well enough to know that it often uses physical imagery to describe things that are beyond our earthbound imaginings. The fires of hell could be like that. But there is nothing here that one should take comfort from. For although the Bible uses imagery to portray the unimaginable, it does so precisely because the reality *is* unimaginable. That is, the suffering of the wicked in hell is so intense and so terrible that, if it is not an actual physical suffering by fire, only such intense physical suffering can be used to describe it.

Do not banter words with Jesus Christ. The point is that hell involves intense suffering. A person is a fool who does not try to avoid that suffering at whatever cost.

The second thing that makes hell terrible is memory, particularly *memory of the blessings of one's previous life*. Though it is not said in Christ's parable about the dragnet, it emerges quite clearly in His parable of the rich man and Lazarus. There Jesus sets up a comparison between a rich man, who "dressed in purple and fine linen and lived in luxury every day" (Luke 16:19), and a beggar named Lazarus, who sat at his gate and longed "to eat what fell from the rich man's table" (v. 21). In time both died. The beggar, being a believer in spite of his unimposing earthly condition, went to heaven. The rich man, in spite of his favored condition on earth, went to hell. Being in torment, the rich man looked up and saw Abraham far away, with Lazarus by his side, and cried out, "Father Abraham, have pity on me and send Lazarus to dip the tip of his finger in water and cool my tongue, because I am in agony in this fire."

But Abraham replied, "Son, *remember* that in your lifetime you received your good things, while Lazarus received bad things, but now he is comforted here and you are in agony" (Luke 16:24-25, emphasis added).

I believe that is one of the most chilling statements in the Bible.

The rich man is told to remember, and what he has to remember is how he enjoyed a lifetime of good things without any reference to God. Now those things are gone, forever. He built his heaven on earth and is never to enter it again, while Lazarus had his taste of hell here and is now to enjoy God's heaven. If you are without Christ, learn that however disappointing you may consider your life to be now, there will, nevertheless, come a day when it will seem "good" compared to your suffering. And the memory of your good things will haunt you and increase your suffering, unless you repent now and come to Jesus.

There is a third thing that will make hell terrible. It is *guilt* over the role the wicked have played in bringing others to their end. More than one hundred years ago, as part of the last great religious awakening to sweep Britain, a man named Brownlow North preached a classic series of revival sermons on the rich man and Lazarus, in one of which he makes that last point well.

He referred to the place where the rich man is said to have interceded for his brothers ("I beg you, father, send Lazarus to my father's house, for I have five brothers. Let him warn them, so that they will not also come to this place of torment," vv. 27-28), and asked how it is that he had suddenly become anxious for his brothers' well-being. It was not because he loved them; there is no love in hell. North believed that it was because of guilt. The rich man was his brothers' keeper, but he had neglected his responsibilities. They had grown up in unbelief like himself, following in his footsteps. Their fate would be like his, and he anticipated how they would reproach him for his role in their destruction. North concluded, "The one thing that can add agony to the agony of the lost is, the being shut up for ever in hell with those they have helped to bring there."[1]

Is that not true? Is Brownlow North not right? You godless fathers, be warned! If you lead your sons along the path you have chosen, they will be present to condemn and curse you in that day. Your agony will be greater because of it.

You mothers, be warned! If you have neglected the spiritual welfare of your daughters, the day will come when you will want to

---

1. Brownlow North, *The Rich Man and Lazarus: A Practical Exposition of Luke 16:19-31* (Edinburgh and Carlisle, Pa.: Banner of Truth, 1979), p. 103.

pray, "Send Lazarus to my daughters," but the time will be past. They will perish, and you will be to blame.

Above all, be warned, all godless ministers! There are ministers who are so ignorant of the God they profess to serve that they never even truly pray. But they will pray in that day. Too late, they will beg God to send someone to warn their congregations. They will have condemned their people by their false gospel and criminal neglect, by their failure to warn them of the wrath to come. North concludes, "I do not believe there exists a more miserable being, even amongst the lost themselves, than a lost minister shut up in hell with his congregation."[2]

A FINAL QUESTION

This study concludes with a question Jesus asked after He had finished telling the parables of the kingdom. He asked, "Have you understood all these things?" (Matt. 13:51). The disciples answered, "Yes."

I find that answer amusing, since the parables of the kingdom have always been one of the most puzzling sections of the Word of God to most readers. Hardly anyone today would dare to say that he or she understands *all* these things. But the disciples thought they did. "Yes," they said, as if the matter was not at all difficult. I must say, however, that I think I know what was involved. Their "yes" did not actually mean that they *understood* all that Jesus was teaching, but only that they at least *believed* all they did understand and were prepared to act upon it.

It is in that sense that I would ask the same question of you: Do you understand these things? No doubt there is much you do not understand, just as there is much I do not understand. But do you believe what you *do* understand? Are you prepared to act upon your understanding and come to Jesus? Just admit that you are a sinner, in rebellion against God, deserving of His judgment. Believe that, in spite of those facts, God has sent His Son to be your Savior. Then commit yourself to Jesus, promising to follow Him as your Master and Lord. Jesus Himself said, "Now that you know these things, you will be blessed if you do them" (John 13:17).

---

2. Ibid., p. 106.

PARABLES OF SALVATION

5

A LOST SHEEP,
A LOST COIN,
A LOST SON

(Luke 15:1-32)

Then Jesus told them this parable: "Suppose one of you has a hundred sheep and loses one of them. Does he not leave the ninety-nine in the open country and go after the lost sheep until he finds it? And when he finds it, he joyfully puts it on his shoulders and goes home. Then he calls his friends and neighbors together and says, 'Rejoice with me; I have found my lost sheep.' I tell you that in the same way there is more rejoicing in heaven over one sinner who repents than over ninety-nine righteous persons who do not need to repent.

"Or suppose a woman has ten silver coins and loses one. Does she not light a lamp, sweep the house and search carefully until she finds it? And when she finds it, she calls her friends and neighbors together and says, 'Rejoice with me; I have found my lost coin.' In the same way, I tell you, there is rejoicing in the presence of the angels of God over one sinner who repents."

Jesus continued: "There was a man who had two sons. The younger one said to his father, 'Father, give me my share of the estate.' So he divided his property between them.

"Not long after that, the younger son got together all he

had, set off for a distant country and there squandered his wealth in wild living. After he had spent everything, there was a severe famine in that whole country, and he began to be in need. So he went and hired himself out to a citizen of that country, who sent him to his fields to feed pigs. He longed to fill his stomach with the pods that the pigs were eating, but no one gave him anything.

"When he came to his senses, he said, 'How many of my father's hired men have food to spare, and here I am starving to death! I will set out and go back to my father and say to him: 'Father, I have sinned against heaven and against you. I am no longer worthy to be called your son; make me like one of your hired men.' So he got up and went to his father.

"But while he was still a long way off, his father saw him and was filled with compassion for him; he ran to his son, threw his arms around him and kissed him.

"The son said to him, 'Father, I have sinned against heaven and against you. I am no longer worthy to be called your son.'

"But the father said to his servants, 'Quick! Bring the best robe and put it on him. Put a ring on his finger and sandals on his feet. Bring the fattened calf and kill it. Let's have a feast and celebrate. For this son of mine was dead and is alive again; he was lost and is found.' So they began to celebrate.

"Meanwhile, the older son was in the field. When he came near the house, he heard music and dancing. So he called one of the servants and asked him what was going on. 'Your brother has come,' he replied, 'and your father has killed the fattened calf because he has him back safe and sound.'

"The older brother became angry and refused to go in. So his father went out and pleaded with him. But he answered his father, 'Look! All these years I've been slaving for you and never disobeyed your orders. Yet you never gave me even a young goat so I could celebrate with my friends. But when this son of yours who has squandered your property with prostitutes comes home, you kill the fattened calf for him!'

" 'My son,' the father said, 'you are always with me, and everything I have is yours. But we had to celebrate and be glad, because this brother of yours was dead and is alive again; he was lost and is found.' "

Among the twenty-seven or so parables of Jesus recorded in the gospels, there are a number that are particularly well known because they deal with salvation. Among those are the three found in Luke 15: the parables of the lost sheep, the lost coin, and the lost son. Bishop J. C. Ryle once said of them, "There is probably no chapter of the Bible that has done greater good to the souls of men." We must make sure that it does good to us as we study it.

An interesting feature of these parables is that they grew out of an attack the self-righteous religious leaders of the day made on Jesus' ministry. Jesus was ministering to society's outcasts: tax collectors, whom everyone hated, and "sinners," which meant those who did not know the law or observe the legal niceties of Pharisaic religion. Jesus freely mingled among such people. He did not despise them, as others did—He loved them. Because He loved them and was attracted to them, it was natural that they loved Him and sought Him out in return. That was noticed and resented by the teachers of the law. They said, "This man welcomes sinners and eats with them" (v. 2). They meant it as a slur on Jesus' reputation, but actually it was part of the great glory of our Lord that He did stoop to save sinners. The three stories are intended to show that it was not only right but also a revelation of the loving character of God the Father that He did so.

In the first two parables, Jesus emphasizes the loss sustained by the owner, his anxious and rigorous search for the object, and his joy when he finds it. In the last parable Jesus teaches the same lesson by portraying the happiness of a father at the return of a rebellious son. In that story emphasis falls on the son's repentance and on the resentful attitude of his older brother, who had remained at home.

I propose to take the stories together, which is how Luke presents them, and focus on the following points: 1. the value of the lost object, 2. the attitude of the owner or father, 3. the nature of the recovery, and 4. the problem with the older son.

VALUABLE TO GOD

The most obvious similarity among these three parables is that in each something has been lost. In the first a sheep is lost, in the second a coin, and in the third a son. This speaks of our miserable condition apart from God.

In each case the object remained valuable in the mind of the owner in spite of its lost condition. We can imagine an owner of sheep who might write off the loss of one sheep lightly. "After all," he might say, "what's one sheep when I still have ninety-nine? The loss is only one percent. A businessman has to expect a certain percentage of loss if he wants to run a business."

Similarly, the woman might have said, "I'm just not going to bother myself about this one lost coin. True, it is one of ten. But I still have nine, and I'm content with them."

The father might have decided, "Well, my younger son is gone, but it's just too bad. Such things happen. I'll focus my attention on the one remaining." Of course, that is not what the owners or the father did. The father longed after his prodigal son, and in the first two parables the owners diligently searched until the lost object was recovered.

What is the explanation for their behavior? Only that the object had value to its owner even though it was lost, and that the owner was determined to recover it again. We do not like to lose anything. If we do, we try to get it back. In these parables Jesus says that God is like us at that point. We are lost. But even in our lost state we retain something of the image of God, and God loves us and is determined to find and reclaim us for the sake of that image.

I am convinced that that is the essential point at which to begin to appreciate these stories. So often we consider them from the point of view of the lostness of the sinner. We think of the misery of the sheep, the hopeless condition of the coin, or the degradation and bondage of the son. But Jesus begins, not with the object's loss, but with the loss sustained by the owners or father, that is, by God. William M. Taylor says that in this alone do we find the infinite pathos of the parables. God "is the shepherd whose sheep has wandered off; *he* is the woman whose piece of money has disappeared in the darkness and debris of the house; *he* is the father whose son has gone away, and become lost to him."[1]

We must be careful here not to suggest that in His divine nature God can in any way be diminished by our sin and rebellion. He is complete with or without us. He does not need us. Still, as Taylor adds, "We dare not eliminate from this losing of the sheep, of the

---

1. William M. Taylor, *The Parables of Our Saviour Expounded and Illustrated* (New York: A. C. Armstrong and Son, 1900), p. 310.

money, of the son, all reference to the feelings of God toward the sinner. They mean that in the separation between him and the man, which sin has caused, Jehovah has lost something which he had formerly possessed and highly valued. They mean that to God the sinner is as something lost is to him to whom it belonged; and these parables let us see how anxious he is and what efforts he will make to regain it for his own."[2]

If you are lost, apart from God, this is the first application of these parables to you: you are valuable to God even in your lost condition. You may be worthless in your own sight because you can only see what you have made of yourself, but you should learn that you are valuable to God because (unlike yourself) He is able to see what you were created to be and what He can yet make of you.

THE SEEKING GOD

In the fifty-third chapter of Isaiah the great prophet of Israel compares sinners to lost sheep: "We all, like sheep, have gone astray, each of us has turned to his own way" (Isa. 53:6). But, as Isaiah goes on to show, God has sought us out even in our lost condition. Jesus became like us, a "sheep [silent] before her shearers" or a "lamb [led] to the slaughter," in order to find us and restore us to God (v. 7).

That is what the Pharisees and teachers of the law failed to see, but it is what Jesus was teaching in the parables. Some have suggested that in these three stories each Person of the Godhead is pictured. In the first Jesus is portrayed in the person of the shepherd. He Himself said, "I am the good shepherd" (John 10:11, 14). In the third parable the divine Father is portrayed in the person of the human father. It is suggested that the Holy Spirit appears in the second parable, in the figure of the woman who lights a lamp, sweeps the house, and carefully searches until the misplaced coin is found. That might suggest the Holy Spirit's work of illumination, but probably it is reading too much into the stories. But the central idea is valid; the entire Godhead is involved in the sinner's salvation. The Father plans the restoration. The Son achieves it by His work on the cross. The Holy Spirit applies it to the individual by opening his or her mind to the truth of the love and work of God and by bringing

---

2. Ibid.

about a repentance that leads the erring one back from the pigsty of sin to the Father's home.

This is our hope—not that we are at work, but that God is at work. He is seeking, and what He seeks he finds. He has said to us, "Ask and it will be given to you; seek and you will find; knock and the door will be opened to you" (Luke 11:9). Are we to believe that God will have less success than ourselves? Jesus said, "The Son of Man came to seek and to save what was lost" (Luke 19:10). Dare we think that the very Son of God will be unsuccessful?

Taken together, it is an amazing picture of God. He is seen grieving, seeking, finding, and rejoicing. That has been true of God's thoughts and actions toward anyone who has ever been found by Jesus. It is true of you if you are a Christian. It will be true of others. A minister named William Jay once called on John Newton, the former slave trader who was strikingly converted while in a storm at sea on his way to England. They were talking about a mutual acquaintance who had recently been converted. Jay observed that the man had once attended on his preaching but that he was an awful character. He said, "He may be converted, though I am not certain of it; but if he is, I shall never despair of the conversion of anyone again."

Newton replied, "I never did since God saved me."

Each Christian has been sought and found by God, who always finds what He seeks. So let no one despair. No matter how great your sins may be, this is the day of grace. The Bible says, "Let the wicked forsake his way and the evil man his thoughts. Let him turn to the LORD, and he will have mercy on him, and to our God, for he will freely pardon" (Isa. 55:7).

LIFE FROM THE DEAD

That brings us to what I have called "the nature of the recovery" and to the last parable in particular. For although it is God who seeks and finds, that is never so apart from the repentance and conversion of the rebellious prodigal. I believe it is chiefly to make that point that Jesus told the third parable.

Here I want to dispose of a common misunderstanding, by looking at each of the parables carefully. The misunderstanding is this: there are people who have looked at the parable of the prodigal son and have imagined, from a consideration of that parable alone, that God is more or less in a hopeless position so far as the salvation of a person is concerned. The son has rebelled. He has squandered his inheritance. He has fallen into bondage in a far country. But in all the story there is no hint that the father does anything. He longs for his son's return, but he does not seek him out. He holds forth no inducements.

Some have supposed, therefore (because of the nature of this story), that in matters of salvation God's hands are tied. He is helpless. On the other hand, it is supposed that the sinner has great powers. It is within him, even in his enslaved state, to come to his senses, cast off his bondage, and return to the Father. That interpretation puts the story of the prodigal son into an entirely different category from the first two parables and even suggests, though gently, that they may be wrong or at least that they are misused when they are interpreted as teaching that salvation is of God.

Some, not willing to say that Scripture can contradict Scripture, suggest that at least the stories teach that people may come to God in different ways. In some cases, God seeks the sinner. In others, the sinner seeks God.

Those are great errors, however, as I have indicated, for if they are read carefully each of the three parables teaches the same thing. True, in the two shorter stories the activity of the seeking God is emphasized, and in the third the nature of repentance and conversion is described. But neither occurs without the other, and that is actually made clear in all three of the parables. It is in the nature of the illustration that Jesus could not picture the repentance of a sheep or coin. Sheep do not repent, nor do coins. But Jesus had that in mind even here, as His concluding comments in each of the two cases show: "I tell you that in the same way there is more rejoicing in heaven over one sinner who repents than over ninety-nine righteous persons who do not need to repent. . . . In the same way, I tell you, there is rejoicing in the presence of the angels of God over one sinner who repents" (vv. 7, 10). In parallel fashion the final parable, though it stresses the human side of salvation, clearly shows that it is not possible apart from God's miraculous intervention and seeking: "This brother of yours was dead and is alive again; he was lost and is found" (v. 32). Only God can produce such a resurrection.

So the two go together. When we say that God finds an individual we mean that by the miracle of regeneration the sinner comes to his senses, repents of sin, and begins to seek God. Or, to put it another way, when we say that a sinner comes to his senses, we mean that God has first sought him out and brought about a spiritual resurrection.

Notice the steps along the way. There were steps away from God: rebellion against the father, desire for total independence, waste of the inheritance, desperate need, debasement, and bondage. It is the way of sin, *always*. But just as there were steps away, so also are there steps back.

First, there is *an awakening to one's true condition* (v. 17). One of the tragedies of sin is that it blinds us to our condition; so we imagine ourselves to be happy when in reality we are miserable, or free when we are enslaved. The most miserable people I know think they are happy, or at least are trying to convince themselves they are happy. If for a moment they do face their condition, they tell themselves that it is only temporary and that sooner or later something will happen to alter it. What has happened is that they have believed the devil's lie: "You will not surely die" (Gen. 3:4). God has told us that "the wages of sin is death" (Rom. 6:23). But they have chosen to believe the devil rather than God and so cover up what is evident to everybody but themselves. The first step in conversion is a recognition and repudiation of the lie, which is actually an awakening to reality.

That is what happened to the prodigal. While he was on his way down he undoubtedly told himself that his hard times were only temporary and that his "ship" would soon come in. He imagined he still had friends. Even when he had to take a job with a detested pig farmer, he supposed he was only doing it on a short-term basis to keep body and soul together until his bad fortune changed. It was only when he was starving to death and recognized that no one, not even his former friends, would give him anything, that he "came to his senses" and acknowledged that he would do better in his father's house as a servant.

The second step in the prodigal's conversion was *an honest confession of true sin*. The son had sinned and now, having come to his senses, he acknowledged his sin: "I will set out and go back to my father and say to him: 'Father, I have sinned against heaven and against you. I am no longer worthy to be called your son; make me like one of your hired men'" (vv. 18-19). Notice that he did not speak of his "youthful wild oats," "faults," or "failings." He did not blame others, as Adam had blamed Eve or Eve the serpent. No! He confessed his *sin*, because sin it was and now he had come to see himself and his offenses clearly. Moreover, he confessed that it was sin "against heaven" as well as against his father, and that gave sin an even greater seriousness. We remember David, who prayed, "Against you, you only, have I sinned and done what is evil in your sight" (Ps. 51:4).

Finally, the third step in his conversion was *an actual return to the father.* Having seen himself as he was and having confessed his sin as sin, the prodigal "got up and went to his father" (v. 20). Thinking alone did not save him, accurate though his thinking was. Confession alone did not save him, though he had much to confess. He needed to turn around and seek God. And that he did! He actually left his sin and returned to his father.

He was going to say, "Make me like one of your hired men," but he did not get a chance to make that petition. Instead, the father showered him with love and declared to the household, "Let's have a feast and celebrate. For this son of mine was dead and is alive again; he was lost and is found" (vv. 23-24).

LIKE GOD OR LIKE SATAN?

But there was one who was not celebrating—the older son. He was out in the field when his younger brother returned home; but when he came in and heard the rejoicing and asked and found out what had happened, he became angry and refused to go in. When the father came out and pleaded with him he answered, "All these years I've been slaving for you and never disobeyed your orders. Yet you never gave me even a young goat so I could celebrate with my friends. But when this son of yours who has squandered your property with prostitutes comes home, you kill the fattened calf for him!" (vv. 29-30).

Many find it easy to sympathize with the older son. I know I do. But I also know that in sympathizing with him I am showing how little like the Father and how much like Satan and the other fallen angels I am. We sympathize with the older son because we think of ourselves as being like him. We are not like the prodigal—so we imagine. We are like that faithful, hardworking, obedient son—so we suppose. But we are not! Or if we are, it is not entirely because we are regenerate but because we have within us the spirit of a hired servant, who works for money, rather than the spirit of a son, who works because he loves his father. What was wrong with the older son? Several things: first, he loved property more than people. He would have been quite happy if the *money* had come back and his *brother* had been lost. As it was, he was angry that the property was lost and his brother recovered. Second, and as a result of his first error, he had an inflated estimate of his own importance and a scorn of others. He was loyal, hardworking, obedient—or so he thought. So low was his opinion of his brother that he would not even acknowledge his relationship to him, calling him only "this son of yours" (v. 30).

That brings the three parables back to the point where they began (vv. 1-2). The Pharisees are the older son. They are those "who were confident of their own righteousness and looked down on everybody else" (Luke 18:9). That also brings the parable back to us, if we consider ourselves better than others or imagine that we are children of the Father because of our character or supposed good works and not purely because of God's good favor.

Will we fault God for acting according to His own gracious nature? If so, he will not accept our accusation. He will acknowledge no wrong on His part. It is right that heaven should rejoice over the repentant sinner; and if we would be like our Father in heaven, we should rejoice also. For the prodigal is our brother, whether or not we acknowledge it. The older son referred to the prodigal as "this son of yours." But the father replied, "We had to celebrate and be glad, because *this brother of yours* was dead and is alive again; he was lost and is found" (v. 32). We are never so like God as when we rejoice at the salvation of sinners. We are never so like Satan as when we despise those who are thus converted and think ourselves superior to them.

6

WORKERS IN THE VINEYARD

(Matthew 20:1-16)

"The kingdom of heaven is like a landowner who went out early in the morning to hire men to work in his vineyard. He agreed to pay them a denarius for the day and sent them into his vineyard.

"About the third hour he went out and saw others standing in the marketplace doing nothing. He told them, 'You also go and work in my vineyard, and I will pay you whatever is right.' So they went.

"He went out again about the sixth hour and the ninth hour and did the same thing. About the eleventh hour he went out and found still others standing around. He asked them, 'Why have you been standing here all day long doing nothing?'

" 'Because no one has hired us,' they answered.

"He said to them, 'You also go and work in my vineyard.'

"When evening came, the owner of the vineyard said to his foreman, 'Call the workers and pay them their wages, beginning with the last ones hired and going on to the first.'

"The workers who were hired about the eleventh hour came and each received a denarius. So when those came who were hired first, they expected to receive more. But each one of them also received a denarius. When they received it, they began to grumble against the landowner. 'These men who were hired last worked only one hour,' they said, 'and you have made them equal to us who have borne the burden of the work and the heat of the day.'

"But he answered one of them, 'Friend, I am not being unfair to you. Didn't you agree to work for a denarius? Take your pay and go. I want to give the man who was hired last the same as I gave you. Don't I have the right to do what I want with my own money? Or are you envious because I am generous?'

"So the last will be first, and the first will be last."

Like any preacher, the Lord Jesus had His favorite sermons. We know because He repeated His words on occasion. Jesus' favorite text is found in slightly different forms in Matthew 18:4; 23:12; Luke 14:11 and 18:14. It is a formula for greatness: "Whoever exalts himself will be humbled, and whoever humbles himself will be exalted" (Matt. 23:12). It is according to this formula, among other things, that Jesus is Himself to be accounted as great, for "He humbled Himself and became obedient to death—even death on a cross! Therefore God exalted Him to the highest place" (Phil. 2:8-9).

The parable now before us—the second of the five parables of salvation—is bracketed by a further variation on the text quoted above. It does not say precisely the same thing, but it is close enough to have come from the same mold. Matthew 19:30 says, "Many who are first will be last, and many who are last will be first" or, in even terser language, "The last will be first, and the first will be last" (Matt. 20:16). Since our parable occupies the fifteen verses between those two statements, they serve as brackets for the story, which must be an illustration of the principle. But who are those who will be last? Who are those who will be first? How can we apply these lessons to our lives?

A DIFFICULT PARABLE

The parable itself is quite simple. A vineyard owner needed men to work in his vineyard, so he went out early in the morning and hired all the workers he could find. He agreed to pay them a denarius (a normal day's wage) for the day's work. Three hours later (that is, about nine in the morning), he went out again and found other workers. He hired them, too, but this time there was no set wage. He merely said, "I will pay you what is right." The new workers agreed with that arrangement and soon joined the others. The owner did the same thing at noon, at three in the afternoon, and at five o'clock, just one hour before quitting time.

At the end of the day he paid the workers, beginning with those he had hired last. He gave each one in that group a denarius, and so on with those hired at three o'clock, noon, and at nine in the morning. At last he came to those who had been hired first. By that time they were rubbing their hands together happily, supposing that if those who had worked less than they had were being paid a denarius, they would receive more. But the owner paid them a denarius too, and they complained. The owner replied, "Friend, I am not being unfair to you. Didn't you agree to work for a denarius? Take your pay and go. I want to give the man who was hired last the same as I gave you. Don't I have the right to do what I want with my own money? Or are you envious because I am generous?" (vv. 13-15).

At that point the parable is followed by the statement mentioned earlier: "So the last will be first, and the first will be last."

The story itself is clear enough, but that does not mean it is without difficulties. The first difficulty is that it presents us with an admittedly strange situation. We have a businessman who is paying people who work only one hour the same wage he is paying those who work all day. We may say, as he does, that the pay for the full day's work is fair. That may be true, but what businessman operates that way? It seems irrational. It produces acute labor problems. More than that, it is bad business. A man who operated like that would soon be bankrupt.

But there is a further difficulty; the payment to the workers seems unjust. We may be reluctant to say it, knowing that the owner of the vineyard is God and that God is always just, regardless of what we may think. But still the procedure *seems* unjust. Why should those who were hired later be paid the same as those who were hired at the start of the day? Why shouldn't those who worked longer be paid more?

There have been many attempts to interpret the parable so as to eliminate difficulties, but those interpretations generally do not work. Some have suggested that those who began early in the day did not work well. They took extended coffee breaks and talked on the job. They knocked off for two-and-a-half hours at lunch. But those who worked a shorter period worked harder. They accomplished as much in their one, four, or seven hours as the early risers did in twelve. It was simply a case of equal pay for equal work. Unfortunately, there is nothing in the story to indicate that, and even much that would go against it. For example, the concluding words stress the generosity of the owner and not his accurate evaluation of the amount of work done (v. 15).

Others have suggested that the coins were different. In one case it was a gold denarius; in another silver, in another bronze, and so on. But, of course, that is mere fantasy. Still others have supposed the parable to be teaching that there are no rewards in heaven and that ultimately it will not matter how much or how little we do for Jesus. The problem with that view is that other biblical texts teach that there *will be* rewards and that our work *does* matter.

So how are we to understand this parable? I believe it is one of a certain class of parables that deal in part with the problems the Jews had when Gentiles began to believe the gospel and embrace Christianity. The problem is reflected in the person of the older son in Jesus' parable of the prodigal (see chapter 5). It is seen in the parable of the banquet, to which many refused to come (Matt. 22), and in the parable of the Pharisee and the tax collector (Luke 18). Above all, it is developed at length in the middle section of Paul's great letter to the Romans (chapters 9-11).

In the earliest days of Old Testament history, from the calling of Abraham about 2,000 years before Christ, God began to deal with the Jews in a special way. It is almost as though He turned His back on the Gentile nations, at least for a time, as He began to create, redeem, and eventually teach and disciple those to whom the Lord Jesus would eventually come. The Jews were quite proud of that heritage, as we ourselves would be.

But instead of remembering that what they were and had accomplished were due entirely to the grace of God (grace that they had often resisted), they began to suppose that the benefits of their position were really due to their own efforts. They thought they had earned their position by many centuries of faithful labor for God. So far there were no complaints; they were glad for the arrangement. But then Jesus came, and even within His lifetime, as well as in a much larger way thereafter, all the benefits the Jews supposed they had earned were offered to Gentiles, who had done nothing to deserve them. They were like the prodigal, who had squandered the father's wealth, or the tax collector, who was utterly immoral to the Jewish way of thinking. In addition to all that, so many Gentiles were being converted that it seemed the cherished Jewish traditions would be overthrown.

As I indicated above, a number of parables deal with the problem — though in a variety of ways. The account of the older brother and the parable of the workers in the vineyard are similar. In each the faithful, hard-working people are resentful of the father's or owner's generosity to those who deserve less. The root problem is *envy*. In the parable of the banquet the diagnosis is somewhat different. In the end the outcasts enter to enjoy the master's banquet, but the reason the ones who were first invited are not there is that *they refused the master's invitation*. In the story of the Pharisee and tax collector the root problem of the self-righteous Pharisee is *pride*.

Those are different ways of analyzing the same problem, a problem that was evident in Jewish reactions to Gentile blessings. But it is not uniquely a Jewish problem. It is a problem for any who think that, because they have served God faithfully for however many years, they deserve something from Him. We never deserve God's favors. If we think we do, we are in danger of losing them entirely.

THREE LESSONS

That brings us to the first clear lesson of the parable: *God is no man's debtor*. It was the opposite claim—that God *is* our debtor—that those who had worked longest wanted to impose on the vineyard owner. They wanted to say that because they had worked twelve hours, and because those who had worked nine or less had been paid a denarius, the owner owed them more than they had originally agreed on. The owner rejected that principle, as does God.

I almost hesitate to use that sentence—God is no man's debtor—because it has been used in a way that is entirely opposite of what I mean by it. I am sure you have heard the argument, which goes like this: "If you put God first and serve Him with all your heart, He will certainly bless you because God is no man's debtor." Or again (in business dealings or other uses of money): "If you put God first, if you give your tithe and then some to the church, God will see that your income goes up and that you become more prosperous than you would have been otherwise, because God is no man's debtor." Used in that way the sentence really means "God is (or can become!) your debtor" because it implies that you can put God in your debt by your actions. That kind of thinking is wrong. The Bible does not teach it, and it is not the lesson I wish to draw from Christ's parable.

When I say that God is no man's debtor I mean that we can never place God under obligation to do something for us because we have done something for Him. There is nothing you or I or anyone else can possibly do that will place God in a debt relationship to us. God owes us nothing except eternal punishment for our sins. So if we do not experience that punishment, that and everything we *do* experience is pure grace. Our Lord taught that truth when He said (in effect), "Your obligation is to work as hard as you possibly can and when you have finished to say, 'At best I am an unprofitable servant' " (cf. Luke 17:10).

Admittedly, it is hard for us to think that way. I remember a story that R. A. Torrey told, growing out of a series of meetings he had held in Melbourne, Australia. He had been speaking on prayer. One day just before a noon meeting a note was placed in his hand. It read:

> Dear Mr. Torrey,
> I am in great perplexity. I have been praying for a long time for something that I am confident is according to God's will, but I do not get it. I have been a member of the Presbyterian church for thirty years, and have tried to be a consistent one all that time. I have been superintendent in the Sunday school for twenty-five years, and an elder in the church for twenty years; and yet God does not answer my prayer and I cannot understand it. Can you explain it to me?

Torrey replied that he could explain it quite easily. He said, "This man thinks that because he has been a consistent church member for thirty years, a faithful Sunday school superintendent for twenty-five years, and an elder in the church for twenty years, that God is under obligation to answer his prayer. He is really praying in his own name, and God will not hear our prayers when we approach him in that way. We must, if we would have God answer our prayers, give up any thought that we have any claims upon God. There is not one of us who deserves anything from God." At the close of the meeting a man came to Torrey, identified himself as the one who had written the note, and said that Torrey had hit the nail squarely on the head. He then confessed his mistake.[1]

That story has to do primarily with prayer, but the principle applies in other areas, too. It applies to anything we do for God and anything we expect from Him. What Jesus' story says is that we have to get over thinking of our service in terms of debt or obligation, and instead learn to serve in the spirit of the son who serves because he loves the father, rather than in the spirit of the hireling who serves only for his wages.

Here God Himself sets the example. This is the second lesson of the parable: *God cares for people more than for things.* Why is it that the owner of the vineyard gave those who had labored only one hour the same amount as those who had labored all day? Was it not because he knew they needed the denarius? When we read the story carefully we notice that not a word of criticism is spoken against those who were not hired in the morning. When the master came and asked them, "Why have you been standing here all day long doing nothing?" they replied, "Because no one has hired us" (vv. 6-7). Apparently they had been willing to work, were eager to work, and undoubtedly needed it. But they had not been hired. We are to think that the owner hired them not for what he could get out of them in just a few hours, but because they needed the work, and that he paid them the full denarius for the same reason. The owner was not thinking of profit. He was thinking of people, and he was using his abundant means to help them.

How different that is from the older son in the parable of Luke 15! He was angered because the father was rejoicing in the return of his younger brother. He should have been rejoicing, too, but instead he was thinking only of how his brother had wasted the inheritance (see Luke 15:29-30). The older brother would have been quite happy if the property had come home and the son had been lost! But as it was, the reverse was true, and he was unhappy. God is just the opposite. He thinks of us far more than of what we can do for Him.

Who are we like? Are we like God in our service, serving because we love Him and not for what He will do for us? Are we like God in our estimate of others, evaluating them in terms of their worth as

1. R. A. Torrey, *The Power of Prayer and the Prayer of Power* (Grand Rapids: Zondervan, 1955), pp. 138-39.

human beings and not merely as tools for production? Or are we like the unhappy workers or the disconsolate older brother?

There is one last point. It comes from the verse with which we began: "But many who are first will be last, and many who are last will be first" (Matt. 19:30). The important word here is "many," for the teaching is not that every person who begins early with God and works for Him throughout a lifetime will inevitably be last or that everyone who begins late will inevitably be first. That will be true for *many* people, but it will not be true for all. Many who begin early will lose their reward (or not even actually come to a true faith in Christ and salvation) because they are approaching God in a false spirit, on the basis of their merit and not on the basis of His grace. Many who enter last will be first because, although they begin late, they nevertheless recognize that their status is due to God's grace alone and praise Him for it. But that is not true for everyone, and for that reason no one is shut up to just those two alternatives.

It is not necessary either to start early and finish last or start last and finish first. In fact, neither is best. The truly desirable thing is to start early and work with all the power at our disposal, not for reward but out of love for our Master, the Lord Jesus Christ, and when we have finished still to say, "We are unprofitable servants." Those are the people God delights to honor.

That is the challenge I would put before you, especially if you are young. Do not wait to serve God. Do not wait until the ninth or eleventh hour of your all-too-brief life. Start now. Serve now. Keep at your service year after year. And when you come to the end say not, "What am I owed for all my service?" but rather, "What a joy it has been to serve such a loving and gracious Lord!"

7

COME TO THE BANQUET

(Matthew 22:1-14)

Jesus spoke to them again in parables, saying: "The kingdom of heaven is like a king who prepared a wedding banquet for his son. He sent his servants to those who had been invited to the banquet to tell them to come, but they refused to come.

"Then he sent some more servants and said, 'Tell those who have been invited that I have prepared my dinner: My oxen and fattened cattle have been butchered, and everything is ready. Come to the wedding banquet.'

"But they paid no attention and went off—one to his field, another to his business. The rest seized his servants, mistreated them and killed them. The king was enraged. He sent his army and destroyed those murderers and burned their city.

"Then he said to his servants, 'The wedding banquet is ready, but those I invited did not deserve to come. Go to the street corners and invite to the banquet anyone you find.' So the servants went out into the streets and gathered all the people they could find, both good and bad, and the wedding hall was filled with guests.

"But when the king came in to see the guests, he noticed a man there who was not wearing wedding clothes. 'Friend,' he asked, 'how did you get in here without wedding clothes?' The man was speechless.

"Then the king told the attendants, 'Tie him hand and foot, and throw him outside, into the darkness, where there will be weeping and gnashing of teeth.'

"For many are invited, but few are chosen."

From time to time in this study I have noted that a particular parable is difficult to interpret, and have mentioned several ways the details of the story could be taken. That problem does not exist with the parable of the wedding banquet, however. On the contrary, it is all too clear. It speaks of God's gracious invitation to us in the gospel and of the indifferent and arrogant way men and women sometimes respond to it. It speaks of hell, the end of those who attempt to enter the king's presence without the wedding garment of Christ's righteousness. Wise is the man or woman who learns from it.

This parable occurs in more than one place and in slightly different form in each place. The fullest form is in Matthew, so we will use Matthew as a starting point. But it also occurs in Luke 14:15-24, which contains elaboration on the excuses of those who refused the king's invitation.

THOSE WHO WOULD NOT COME

The story begins with a certain king who prepared a wedding banquet for his son, and sent servants to those who had been invited to tell them that the feast was now ready and that they should come. But they refused to come. Their refusal was a great insult, of course. It was dishonoring to the son, the king, and even to the servants who carried the king's message. But the king did not get angry. Instead, he sent other servants to repeat the invitation: "Tell those who have been invited that I have prepared my dinner: My oxen and fattened cattle have been butchered, and everything is ready. Come to the wedding banquet" (v. 4). Again they refused, but this time, those who had been invited did not merely reject the invitation. They also mistreated the messengers and killed some of them. The king sent an army to destroy the murderers and burn their city (vv. 1-7). After that he invited others.

The thing that makes the parable so easy to understand is that nearly every part is discussed in plain terms elsewhere. The king is God, sitting upon the throne of the universe. The son is His Son, the Lord Jesus Christ. The messengers are the prophets and early preachers of the gospel. The banquet is the marriage supper of the Lamb. Those to whom the gospel was first preached were Jews and those who actually came to the banquet were Gentiles, as is taught in John 1:11-12. "He came to that which was his own, but his own did not receive him. Yet to all who received him, to those who believed in his name, he gave the right to become children of God."

As with the preceding parable, this is one of a special class of parables that deals with the refusal of Israel to respond to the Lord Jesus Christ when He came first to His own people. That was a major issue during the lifetime of the Lord, as well as afterward, so it is not surprising to find a number of parables dealing with it either directly or alluding to it indirectly. The character of the older son in the parable of the prodigal represents Israel (as well as those Gentiles who possess the same spirit of resentment). So do those workers in the vineyard who were hired early but were paid the same as those who came late. So does the Pharisee in the parable of the Pharisee and the tax collector (Luke 18). Those stories explore the thinking of people who supposed they had worked long and faithfully for God, unlike others, and who were envious and resentful when the grace of God was shown to those they considered unworthy.

The unique element in the parable before us is the willful refusal of those who were invited. It was not that they *could* not come. Rather, they *would* not. The reason for their refusal is not spelled out, but it is suggested in the way the servants were treated. They "seized" the servants, "mistreated them and killed them" (v. 6). If the invited guests felt that way toward the servants, they obviously felt that way toward the king who had sent them and would have seized, mistreated, and killed him if they could have. In other words, they would not come because they actually despised the king and were hostile to him.

Those of Christ's day bitterly resented His portrait of them, but resent it or not, that is precisely the way those religious leaders thought and acted. In the chapter immediately preceding (Matt. 21:33-46), Jesus told of tenant farmers who beat, killed, and stoned the owner's servants. At last they murdered his son. In the chapter following (Matt. 23), Jesus pronounces "woes" upon those same people, saying,

"Woe to you, teachers of the law and Pharisees, you hypocrites! You build tombs for the prophets and decorate the graves of the righteous. And you say, 'If we had lived in the days of our forefathers, we would not have taken part with them in shedding the blood of the prophets.' So you testify against yourselves that you are the descendants of those who murdered the prophets. Fill up, then, the measure of the sin of your forefathers! . . . I am sending you prophets and wise men and teachers. Some of them you will kill and crucify; others you will flog in your synagogues and pursue from town to town. And so upon you will come all the righteous blood that has been shed on earth, from the blood of righteous Abel to the blood of Zechariah son of Berakiah, whom you murdered between the temple and the altar. . . . O Jerusalem, Jerusalem, you who kill the prophets and stone those sent to you, how often I have longed to gather your children together, as a hen gathers her chicks under her wings, but you were not willing." [Matt. 23:29-37]

We know that at the last those rebellious subjects of the King of heaven killed Christ. As Stephen later put it, "Was there ever a prophet your fathers did not persecute? They even killed those who predicted the coming of the Righteous One. And now you have betrayed and murdered him—you who have received the law that was put into effect through angels but have not obeyed it" (Acts 7:52-53).

Today we are not so inclined to kill prophets. But if we are honest, we will admit that the same spirit is present among many of our contemporaries and that they and others sometimes dispose of God's messengers by ridicule or neglect, if not by more violent hostility. Charles H. Spurgeon preached seven sermons on this parable during the course of his long ministry, and he was deeply touched by that fact. He said,

> Today this same class will be found among the children of godly parents; dedicated from their birth, prayed for by loving piety, listening to the gospel from their childhood, and yet unsaved. We look for these to come to Jesus. We naturally hope that they will feast upon the provisions of grace, and like their parents will rejoice in Christ Jesus; but, alas! how often it is the case they will not come! . . . A preacher may be too rhetorical:

let a plain-speaking person be tried. He may be too weighty: let another come with parable and anecdote. Alas! with some of you the thing wanted is not a new voice, but a new heart. You would listen no better to a new messenger than to the old one.[1]

Some who are invited to the gospel banquet do not openly express their hatred of the one who gives it, but they make excuses. As the parable says, they go off "one to his field, another to his business" (v. 5). Jesus elaborates that point in Luke's version of the parable. There he says, "But they all alike began to make excuses. The first said, 'I have just bought a field, and I must go and see it. Please excuse me.'

"Another said, 'I have just bought five yoke of oxen, and I'm on my way to try them out. Please excuse me.'

"Still another said, 'I just got married, so I can't come'" (Luke 14:18-20). Each of those excuses is trifling. As Jesus tells it, it is not a case of a man's being on his deathbed, unable to move, nor a woman's being kept at home by a violent husband. Not one of their excuses has any weight at all. So what if a man had just bought a field? There is no reason why he would have had to see it on that particular day and so miss the banquet. The field would wait. There was no reason why the second person had to try out his oxen. They would keep. Even the excuse about marriage had no weight. Are we to think that a new bride would be unwelcome at a feast to which her husband had been invited?

Besides that, the invitation was not the first they had received. In both versions of the parable Jesus speaks of an invitation to those who had *already* been invited. That is, the invitations had already been sent out. There was no excuse for the guests to have failed in arranging their schedules accordingly. When the final summons came they should have been anticipating the festivities eagerly.

Many who reject the gospel invitation today have equally flimsy excuses and will rightly incur the King's wrath. They say they are too busy for spiritual things. They say they have fields or patients or bonds or whatever it is that imprisons their souls and keeps them from faith in Him who brings salvation. Spurgeon, whom I quoted earlier, tells of a rich ship owner who was visited by a godly man. The

1. Charles Haddon Spurgeon, "The Wedding Was Furnished with Guests," in *The Metropolitan Tabernacle Pulpit,* vols. 28-37 (London: Banner of Truth, 1970), 34:254-55.

Christian asked, "Well, sir, what is the state of your soul?" to which the merchant replied, "Soul? I have no time to take care of my soul. I have enough to do just taking care of my ships." But he was not too busy to die, which he did about a week later.[2]

Do you fit that pattern? Are you more interested in your good credit than in Christ? Do you read the stock quotations more than you read your Bible? You do not have to murder a prophet to miss out. You have only to fritter away your time on things that will eventually pass away and thus let your opportunitites for repentance pass by.

THOSE WHO CAME

Half the parable (Matt. 22:1-7) is about those who despised the king and would not come to the banquet. But there is a second half (vv. 8-14), which tells of those who did come. The king instructed, "Go to the street corners and invite to the banquet anyone you find" (v. 9). In Luke that is elaborated to show how those persons were drawn from the lower ranks of life. "Go out quickly into the streets and alleys of the town and bring in the poor, the crippled, the blind and the lame. . . . Go out to the roads and country lanes and make them come in, so that my house will be full" (Luke 14:21, 23).

In terms of Christ's story that seems an extraordinary thing for the king or master of the house to have done. But when we think in terms of God it seems inevitable. We ask these questions: Is it possible that God, the King of the universe, can be dishonored by having no one at the wedding supper of His Son? Can the almighty God be defeated? Disappointed? Can the work of God's Son, the Lord Jesus Christ, prove ineffective? Can Jesus have died in vain? Risen in vain? Ascended in vain? If He did all that and yet no one receives salvation through faith in His completed work, is He not dishonored? Would Satan not have triumphed? Would the demons not have taunted Him: "He saved Himself; His own He cannot save"? To put the questions in that way shows the impossibility of such an outcome. God must be honored. Jesus must be effective in His saving work. As Jesus Himself said, "All that the Father gives me *will* come to me, and whoever comes to me I will never drive away" (John 6:37, emphasis added).

2. Charles Haddon Spurgeon, "Making Light of Christ," in *The New Park Street Pulpit,* Vols. 1-6 (Pasadena, Tex.: Pilgrim Publications, 1975), 2:358.

"But surely God is dishonored by the kinds of people who do come," someone may say. "Those are not the noble people who were first invited. They are not wise, not mighty." True. As Paul says, "God chose the foolish things of the world to shame the wise; God chose the weak things of the world to shame the strong. He chose the lowly things of this world and the despised things—and the things that are not—to nullify the things that are, so that no one may boast before him" (1 Cor. 1:27-29). But God is not dishonored thereby. On the contrary, He is most highly honored.

How is God honored? Let me share Spurgeon's answer to that question:

> *The persons who came to the wedding were more grateful* than the first invited might have been if they had come. The richer sort had a good dinner every day. Those farmers could always kill a fat sheep, and those merchants could always buy a calf. "Thank you for nothing," they would have said to the king if they had accepted his invitation. But these poor beggars picked off the streets . . . welcomed the fatlings. How glad they were! One of them said to the other, "It's a long time since you and I sat down to such a joint as this," and the other answered, "I can hardly believe that I am really in a palace dining with a king. Why, yesterday I begged all the day and only had twopence at night. Long live the king, say I, and blessings on the prince and his bride!" I warrant, they were thankful for such a feast. . . .
>
> *The joy that day was much more expressed* than it would have been had others come. Those ladies and gentlemen who were first invited, if they had come to the wedding, would have seated themselves there in a very stiff and proper manner. . . . But these beggars! They make a merry clatter; they are not muzzled by propriety; they are glad at the sight of every dish. . . .
>
> *The occasion became more famous* than it would otherwise have been. If the feast had gone on as usual it would have been only one among many such things; but now this royal banquet was the only one of its kind, unique, unparalleled. To gather in poor men off the streets, labouring men and idle men, bad men and good men, to the wedding of the Crown Prince—this was a new thing under the sun. Everybody talked of it. There were

songs made about it, and these were sung in the king's honor where none honored kings before. . . . Dear friends, when the Lord saved some of us by his grace, it was no common event. When he brought us great sinners to his feet, and washed us, and clothed us, and fed us, and made us his own, it was a wonder to be talked of for ever and ever. We will never leave off praising his name throughout eternity. That which looked as though it would defame the King turned out to his honor, and "the wedding was furnished with guests."[3]

Ultimately, nothing will ever dishonor God. Nor will His work of salvation, upon which His glory chiefly rests, be seen to be imperfect.

THE MAN WITHOUT A GARMENT

At this point the parable seems to be over. But it is not, and I am glad, because the Lord goes on to give a much-needed warning in the account of the man who came to the feast without a wedding garment. I say it is needed because there is sometimes a kind of inverse pride found in the disadvantaged that imagines that, because they are not rich or famous or powerful but poor and unknown and weak, therefore, they *deserve* the king's bounty and can come before Him in their own character and on the basis of their own "good" works. Jesus exposed that error by showing how the man who came to the feast without a garment was immediately confronted by the king and then thrown "outside, into the darkness, where there will be weeping and gnashing of teeth" (v. 13).

What is the wedding garment? It is the righteousness of Christ, provided freely to all who will repent of sin and trust in the Lord Jesus Christ for salvation. We sing of it in one of our hymns:

> Jesus, thy blood and righteousness
> My beauty are, my glorious dress;
> 'Midst flaming worlds, in these arrayed,
> With joy shall I lift up my head.

If we are clothed in that righteousness, we will be able to stand before God and rejoice in our salvation. If we are not clothed in it, we will be speechless before Him.

---

3. Spurgeon, "The Wedding," pp. 261-63.

I am interested in that detail—"the man was speechless"—because that is the same thought Paul expresses in Romans 3:19 when he says that "every mouth [will] be silenced and the whole world held accountable to God." During the long years of his ministry, Donald Grey Barnhouse developed a way of presenting the gospel that used that text. When he was speaking to a person who was not sure he was a Christian, Barnhouse would ask, "Suppose you should die tonight and appear before God in heaven and He should ask you, 'What right do you have to come into My heaven?', what would you say?" Barnhouse had learned from experience that there were only three possible answers a person might give.

Many would cite their good works, saying, "Well, I'd say I've done the best I can, and I've never done anything particularly bad." That is an appeal to one's record. But, as Barnhouse pointed out, our record is one of sin and thus "no one will be declared righteous in [God's] sight by observing the law" (Rom. 3:20). It is our record that got us into trouble in the first place.

A second group of people would respond as did a woman whom Barnhouse once met on a ship crossing the Atlantic. He asked, "If God demanded of you, 'What right do you have to come into My heaven?', what would you say?"

She responded, "I wouldn't have a thing to say." In other words, she would be "speechless." Her "mouth [would] be silenced and [she would be] held accountable to God." Jesus says that will be the case of all when God actually does ask that question. In this life we may get by with the delusion that our record is pretty good and that God will be satisfied with it. But in that day, when we see God in His glory and understand what true righteousness is, our folly will be apparent to ourselves as well as to all other beings in the universe, and we will be reduced to silence—if we are not clothed with the wedding garment of our Lord's own righteousness.

That is the third and only acceptable answer, of course. "What right do you have to come into My heaven?"

"None at all, so far as I myself am concerned. But Jesus died for my sins and has given me the covering of His own righteousness in which alone I dare to stand before You. I come at Your invitation and in that clothing." Will God reject such a one? He will not, for it is such persons He has bid come to Him.

8

THE NARROW DOOR
OF SALVATION

(Luke 13:22-30)

Then Jesus went through the towns and villages, teaching as he made his way to Jerusalem. Someone asked him, "Lord, are only a few people going to be saved?"

He said to them, "Make every effort to enter through the narrow door, because many, I tell you, will try to enter and will not be able to. Once the owner of the house gets up and closes the door, you will stand outside knocking and pleading, 'Sir, open the door for us.'

"But he will answer, 'I don't know you or where you come from.'

"Then you will say, 'We ate and drank with you, and you taught in our streets.'

"But he will reply, 'I don't know you or where you come from. Away from me, all you evildoers!'

"There will be weeping there, and gnashing of teeth, when you see Abraham, Isaac and Jacob and all the prophets in the kingdom of God, but you yourselves thrown out. People will come from east and west and north and south, and will take their places at the feast in the kingdom of God. Indeed there are those who are last who will be first, and first who will be last."

Most of what we have called parables of salvation are obvious parables. The parable of the narrow door, recorded in Luke 13:22-30, should probably be called a borderline parable, if it is one at all. I mean that it is not truly a story. It is more a response of Jesus to a question He was asked. He answered by an illustration that became a story, though it did not start out to be one. Jesus was asked whether only a few people would be saved, and He responded by telling His questioner, "Make every effort to enter through the narrow door, because many, I tell you, will try to enter and will not be able to" (v. 24). He then told how the owner of the house was going to get up and close the door, and created some dialogue to go along with the setting.

The reason for considering that amplified illustration as a parable is that it is an important picture of our Lord's teaching about salvation and thus occurs in many places, even as a part of other parables. The Sermon on the Mount has a similar illustration. As the Lord came to the end of that address He admonished His listeners, "Enter through the narrow gate. For wide is the gate and broad is the road that leads to destruction, and many enter through it. But small is the gate and narrow the road that leads to life, and only a few find it" (Matt. 7:13-14). In that passage, the narrow door is contrasted with a broad one, and a broad and a narrow path are added to the basic image.

The same idea occurs toward the end of Matthew in the parable of the five wise and five foolish virgins. There the bridegroom comes, and the door is shut. No amount of crying on the part of the foolish maidens gets the bridegroom to open the door again (Matt. 25:1-13). The image is also found in John in the portrait of the sheep and their shepherd: "I am the gate for the sheep," and "I am the gate" (John 10:7, 9).

Of those varied settings in which the illustration of the narrow door occurs, none is as interesting as that of Luke 13. The reason is the question that begins the section: "Lord, are only a few people going to be saved?" I do not know what kind of an answer you might have expected the Lord to give to that question if you had been there, but I imagine you would have expected a simple yes or no. "Are only a few people going to be saved? Well, what is it, Lord? Is it going to be few or many? Tell us. We want to know."

But Jesus did not answer the question that way. The reason He did not is that it was mere theological speculation. So far as Jesus was concerned, the answer was irrelevant. The only thing that mattered was whether the questioner himself would be among the number of the saved, whether small or large. So the Lord answered the question by not answering it. He said instead, "Your duty (and the part of wisdom) is to get through that door. You can worry about the size of the heavenly hotel later. Right now your exclusive and compelling concern should be to get through that door so you will be on the right side when it closes and judgment comes."

That is what Jesus says to us also. That is the message of this parable. I break it down into three parts: 1. There is only one door, and it is a narrow one; 2. that door is now open, though it will one day close; and 3. our duty is to enter it.

I AM THE DOOR

The first of those—the truth that lies at the heart of Christ's illustration—is that salvation is by faith in the Lord Jesus Christ alone. That is what the imagery of the door is all about. What is the door? "What is the way that leads to life? The answer is: Jesus Christ. He said, "I am the gate for the sheep. All who ever came before me were thieves and robbers; but the sheep did not listen to them. I am the gate; whoever enters through me will be saved" (John 10:7-9). Again, "I am the way and the truth and the life. No one comes to the Father except through me" (John 14:6). Those verses throw light on and give the only proper interpretation to our text.

That is crucial for Christianity, but not so for other religions. It would make little difference to most of the world's religions if their founder were someone else, or even if they had no founder at all, for essentially they are collections of spiritual truths (or claims to truth) and methods, all of which could exist without their founder. They needed someone to discover them, of course. But anyone could have done that, and once they are discovered they exist in their own right much like scientific propositions. Besides, if they become lost, they can always be rediscovered.

That is the nature of the world's religions. Christianity is not in that category, however. Nor is Jesus like those other religious figures. Jesus did not merely show the way to God; He said, "I *am* the way." He did not claim merely to know the truth; He said, "I *am* the truth."

He did not merely point to the abundant life; He said, "I *am* the life." Therefore, within Christianity if there is no Christ, there is no way to God, no truth about God, and no vitality.

How could Jesus make such claims? If He was only a man, His claims are preposterous. But if He is who He said He is, and if He did what He said He would do, His claims make sense. Jesus claimed to be God and to have come to earth to die for our sin. We deserve to die for our own sin, but Jesus died in our place. He who was sinless accepted the guilt of our sin and died for us. No one else could do it, but He could and did. Thus, He literally became the door by which sinful men and women can approach the Father. The author of the book of Hebrews called Him "a new and living way" (10:20). Paul wrote, "Through him we . . . have access to the Father" (Eph. 2:18).

That means, among other things, that no one will ever come to God through nature. That is a popular thought among many who are dissatisfied with Christian churches, but the idea that God can be found in nature is an illusion; it leads to idolatry.

Once, after I had spoken on the subject, a woman told me of her experiences witnessing on the beaches of California. In many cases surfers told her that they worshiped God in nature. She soon learned to ask, "What is God?" Often she was told, "My surfboard is my god," or something like it. That is honest, at least, but pure paganism. A person is self-deluded to think that such an attitude has anything to do with the worship of God Almighty, the Father of the Lord Jesus Christ. We do not worship God in nature by playing golf on Sunday morning or going for a drive in the country. If you are doing that, you are either not worshiping at all, which is probably most often the case, or you are worshiping nature. But nature is not God! That belief is pantheism.

The Bible says that the revelation of God in nature condemns us for our failure to recognize Him. Romans 1:18-20 says that "the wrath of God" is being revealed from heaven against all people because "since the creation of the world God's invisible qualities—his eternal power and divine nature—have been clearly seen, being understood from what has been made, so that men are without excuse." No one has ever come to our Lord Jesus Christ through nature alone.

No one finds God in mere pious thoughts or religion, either. That is, we will not find God in the mere performance of religious duties, whether the fourfold or sevenfold path to Nirvana, a life of meditation, the "religion" of drugs, or even the ceremonial aspects of Christianity. God has written *no* over all human efforts to be religious in order that He might write a *yes* over all who abandon religion and turn to Him in Christ. Religion is your seeking after a god in your own image. Christianity is God's seeking you and moving to redeem you by the death of His Son.

Lastly, no one can find God through morality by attempting to live up to God's standards or even his own. We fall short of *all* standards. The first three chapters of Romans are written to show that no one will find God in any way but through Christ, and that includes the person with high moral standards. Paul describes the different types of persons—the pagan, moralist, and religious person—and then concludes that all are condemned:

> There is no one righteous, not even one;
> There is no one who understands,
>   no one who seeks God;
> All have turned away,
>   they have together become worthless;
> There is no one who does good,
>   not even one.
>
> Rom. 3:10-12

Our natural ways are not real ways to God.

But there is a way. You and I have sinned, in little ways or in big ways (it does not matter), and sin keeps us from God. Unless sin is removed we shall never get into God's heaven. How can sin be removed? Jesus has removed it for us by becoming our substitute. He died, not for His own sin (because He did not have any), but for your sin and mine. God will not punish the same sin twice. Therefore, if you believe that Jesus died for you, if you acknowledge Him as your substitute, God has removed your sin forever by punishing it on the cross of Jesus, and it is correct to say that you have passed along the narrow way through the narrow door to salvation.

Do not make the mistake of counting on your moral record as a way of coming to God. It is your record that gets you into trouble in the first place. Your record will condemn you, no matter how good you think you are or how good you appear in other people's eyes. Count on the fact that Jesus paid the penalty for your sin, and accept the fact that He is the way for simple, sinful people like you and me to enter heaven.

THE DOOR IS OPEN

The first lesson of Jesus' parable of the door is two-fold: there is only one door and it is a narrow one. But there is a second lesson that is correspondingly broad: anyone may enter it. The time is coming when the door will be closed and locked. The time for repentance is not endless. But there is time for repentance now, while the door is open. Today anyone may enter and be saved.

That truth has sometimes been taken as contradicting John 6:44, which says: "No one can come to me unless the Father who sent me draws him." But that is a mistaken inference. Those who dislike John 6:44 either disregard it or try to use the gospel invitation to overturn its plain meaning. Actually the two verses are not in conflict. John 6:44 looks at the matter from the Godward side and declares, quite rightly, that no one ever made the first move toward God. We come to God only because God draws us. On the other hand, as the texts about the open door show, God does not show favoritism. Anyone, regardless of who he or she is or where he or she comes from, may be among that number.

The call of God is not restricted by anything you can imagine: race, education, social position, wealth, achievements, good deeds, the lack of them, or anything else. Therefore, there is no reason why you (whoever you are) should not be among the number of those whom God draws to Jesus.

But you must enter by the door. To enter is not hard; there is no complicated course to follow. If Jesus had compared Himself to a wall, we would have to climb over, and it might be hard work. If He had compared Himself to a long, dark passageway, we would have to feel our way along it, and some might be afraid to try. But Jesus said He was a *door,* and a door can be entered easily and instantly. But it must be entered. There is no way of getting around that.

Let me demonstrate what we must do by this story. A number of years ago a woman sat in a pew in the Tenth Presbyterian Church in Philadelphia, where I now serve as pastor. At the time, the pastor was Donald Grey Barnhouse. He was talking about the cross and the need to believe on the Christ who died on it. The woman was not a Christian. She had been raised in a religious home and had heard about Jesus. But she did not understand those things and therefore obviously had never actually trusted in Jesus.

As Barnhouse spoke of the cross he said, "Imagine that the cross is a door or that it has a door in it. All you are asked to do is to go through. On one side, the side facing you, there is an invitation: 'Whosoever will may come.' You stand there with your sin upon you and wonder if you should enter or not. Finally you do, and as you do the burden of your sin drops away. You are safe and free. Joyfully you then turn around and see written on the backside of the cross, through which you have now entered, the words: 'Chosen in Him before the foundation of the world.' " Barnhouse invited those who were listening to enter.

The woman later said that it was the first time in her life she had really understood what it meant to be a Christian and that, in understanding it, she had believed. She believed right there—in that church at that moment. She entered the door. Moreover, her life then bore witness to the fact that a great change had occurred and that she was God's child. I am certain of the facts of my story because that woman is my mother.

Jesus said, "Whoever enters through me will be saved" (John 10:9). That includes you, and it refers to something that can take place now. If you have not yet trusted Jesus, You can trust Him now. Today is the day of salvation.

STRIVE TO ENTER

There is one last point to this parable, found in the word with which Jesus introduces His answer to the original question. It is the Greek word *agōnizomai,* from which we get our word "agonize." It means to "strive" (KJV) or to "make every effort" (NIV). By this word Jesus tells us that there is something for us to do in the matter of salvation and that we must make it our supreme business to do it.

That creates a theological problem, of course, for it seems to say that we can contribute to our salvation. Earlier I said that Jesus is the only way of salvation. But if we are to strive to enter by that one door, are we not in some sense the way, too? Do we not actually contribute something? Or if we do not, what does Jesus mean by striving or making every effort to enter?

Here we are helped by a way of speaking that was quite common at certain periods of church history, but which is not common today and should be revived. It is what Jonathan Edwards called "preparation for salvation." He did not mean by it that there is anything we can do to make God look favorably on us, because there is not. He did not mean that we can regenerate ourselves, even by employing the most rigorous means. He also did not mean that we can draw ourselves to God, because it is God who draws us, and unless God draws none can come to Him (John 6:44). Edwards meant rather that although it is absolutely true that you cannot save yourself or even truly seek God, it is nevertheless also true that you can lay aside those things that would normally fill your heart and mind to the exclusion of spiritual matters, and in their place put those "means of grace" through which God normally draws men and women to Himself.

For example, you can read the Bible. You can expose yourself to Christian teaching. You can fellowship with God's people. You can even pray—not pretending to have a relationship with God you do not have but rather praying something like this: "God, I do not know that I like You and there are even times when I doubt that You exist. But in my better moments I know You must be there and that I have to come to terms with you sooner or later, and therefore preferably sooner. That is what I am trying to do. I want to do everything I can do, not thinking that I can save myself or regenerate myself—I know salvation is Your business—but by exposing myself to Your truth and whatever means of grace You've made available. I want You to save me in spite of myself. Amen."

Even a prayer like that does not put God under obligation to you. But if you can pray it honestly, it is at least an encouraging sign. If nothing else, you are at least not sinning more but are instead obeying Christ who told you to strive. And you can have hope that God will speak to you and draw you to Himself. I can tell you this: salvation does not come in any other way. It does not come from the world and its values, nor from the world's books. It comes from God through the means He has provided. If you have not yet done so, may God give you the grace to move vigorously in that direction.

9

THE PHARISEE AND THE TAX COLLECTOR

(Luke 18:9-14)

To some who were confident of their own righteousness and looked down on everybody else, Jesus told this parable: "Two men went up to the temple to pray, one a Pharisee and the other a tax collector. The Pharisee stood up and prayed about himself: 'God, I thank you that I am not like all other men— robbers, evildoers, adulterers—or even like this tax collector. I fast twice a week and give a tenth of all I get.'

"But the tax collector stood at a distance. He would not even look up to heaven, but beat his breast and said, 'God, have mercy on me, a sinner.'

"I tell you that this man, rather than the other, went home justified before God. For everyone who exalts himself will be humbled, and he who humbles himself will be exalted."

The story of the Pharisee and the tax collector is among the best-known and best-loved of Christ's parables—right alongside the parables of the Good Samaritan and the Prodigal Son. But it is often misunderstood. On the surface it is a story about two men and their prayers, which might lead one to think that it is essentially about prayer. Actually, it is a parable of salvation. The prayers embody two contrasting approaches to God, one on the basis of the individual's supposed good works and the other on the basis of God's mercy made known through the system of sacrifices. The conclusion is that a person is justified by the second approach only.

Justification! That is the key word and the clue to the parable's meaning. Jesus did not say, after telling of the prayer of the tax collector, "I tell you that this man, rather than the other, had his prayer answered." He said rather, "This man, rather than the other, went home *justified* before God" (v. 14). So the parable answers the question: How is a person to be justified before God?

Martin Luther called justification the "chief article" of Christian theology. He wrote, "This is the chief article from which all our other doctrines have flowed." He also argued, "It alone begets, nourishes, builds, preserves, and defends the church of God; and without it the church of God cannot exist for one hour." He believed that "when the article of justification has fallen, everything has fallen." He called justification "the master and prince, the lord, the ruler, and the judge over all kinds of doctrines."[1]

John Calvin was less rhetorical, but he called justification "the main hinge on which religion turns."[2] Thomas Watson, the Puritan, wrote, "Justification is the very hinge and pillar of Christianity. An error about justification is dangerous, like a defect in a foundation. Justification by Christ is a spring of the water of life. To have the poison of corrupt doctrine cast into this spring is damnable."[3]

That is not hyperbole. It is simple truth. We are not right with God. We are alienated from Him and are under His wrath. How we escape that wrath and become reconciled to God is the essential issue.

A SHOCKING CONTRAST

The Lord's story is based on a contrast, as we have already intimated. But it is a contrast on two levels. The first contrast is between the Pharisee and the tax collector themselves. The second is between a normal human judgment on their acceptability before God and God's judgment.

When Jesus began His story by introducing two men, "one a

1. Martin Luther, *What Luther Says: An Anthology,* comp. Ewald M. Plass, 3 vols. (St. Louis: Concordia, 1959), 2:702-4, 715.
2. John Calvin, *Institutes of the Christian Religion,* ed. John T. McNeill, and trans. Ford Lewis Battles, 2 vols. (Philadelphia: Westminster, 1960), 1:726.
3. Thomas Watson, *A Body of Divinity* (London: Banner of Truth, 1970), p. 226.

Pharisee, and the other a tax collector," He made a contrast that those of His time would readily visualize. We have a bad mental image of Pharisees because of some of the things Jesus said, but that was not the case in His day, for the most part. The Pharisees were the most highly regarded of the various sects of Judaism. To begin with, there were never very many of them. At the most there were only about three thousand at any one time. Besides, they were not political figures essentially, although they had great political power due to their being so highly regarded. They were a religious body whose chief concern was to observe the most minute points of the law. Nicodemus was a Pharisee. So was Paul. Those men were among the most honored of their contemporaries.

But who was the other person in Christ's parable? He was a tax collector—"a no-good, money-grubbing, cheating, Roman collaborator," as most of the people of that day would have called him. Tax collectors were Jews empowered by the Roman government to collect all the taxes they could. They were permitted to keep any excess above what the government required. So they were not loved, but despised. People would cross the street to pass on the other side when they saw a tax collector coming. So when Jesus spoke of two men, a Pharisee and a tax collector, it was as though He had spoken of the Chief Justice of the Supreme Court and a rapist, or the President of the United States and a prostitute.

Moreover, that initial comparison and the mental picture it conveyed was heightened by what the Lord went on to say. He tells how the Pharisee "stood [up] and was praying"—as everyone would agree he had every right to do. Why should he not stand up? If he did not, he would probably be invited to: "Come here, Mr. Pharisee. Stand where we can all hear you. Everyone be quiet now; the Pharisee is going to pray." So the Pharisee threw out his chest, collected his thoughts, and prayed about himself. He prayed, "God, I thank you that I am not like other men—robbers, evildoers, adulterers—or even like this tax collector. I fast twice a week and give a tenth of all I get" (vv. 11-12). I do not think he was lying. I think he really did give a tenth of his income to the Temple. I think he really did fast twice a week. Surely he was not an adulterer, an evildoer (as he understood it), or a robber. Moreover, I think other people would have concurred in that evaluation. They would have regarded him as a most outstanding man, a leader in his community, the kind of person they wanted to get on their boards of reference or invite to their homes for dinner. They would have been pleased just to know him, not to mention actually having him as a friend.

Then there was that other person, the tax collector. Jesus tells how he "stood at a distance"—where he belonged. If they had had buses in those days, he would have belonged at the back of the bus. He certainly did not belong up front with the "good" people. In addition, when he prayed, "he would not even look up to heaven, but beat his breast and said, 'God, have mercy on me, a sinner'" (v. 13). And why not? He *was* a sinner. He had plenty to beat his breast about.

It is hard to imagine a greater contrast. As to occupation, noble versus base. As to bearing, proud versus shameful. As to self-evaluation, self-confident versus cringing. Yet as the Lord concludes the parable He reverses the judgment that everyone would undoubtedly have been making, concluding of the tax collector, "I tell you that this man, rather than the other, went home justified before God. For everyone who exalts himself will be humbled, and he who humbles himself will be exalted" (v. 14).

No dime-store novel, no cinematic melodrama ever had a more surprising ending than this parable.

"ME, A SINNER"

The Lord's evaluation of those two men and their prayers is so contrary, not only to what those of His day thought but also to what those of our day think, that it is almost demanded of us that we go back and take a second look at the characters. We have presented the story as Christ told it, but perhaps we have been overly hasty in our evaluation. True, the first man was a Pharisee and was therefore quite highly regarded. But we have been looking only on the surface, after all. He claimed to give a tenth of his income to religious work, but perhaps that was not actually the case. Perhaps, like Ananias and Sapphira, he was keeping back a portion. He claimed to fast twice each week, but who knows what he did in the privacy of his own home? Perhaps he cheated. So far as adultery is concerned, perhaps he cheated there as well. Perhaps he really was a robber or evildoer. Or perhaps he had committed some other sin that no one but himself and the Lord knew about. Perhaps it is for those things that he went away unjustified.

Or again, there is the tax collector. He was certainly in a bad profession; no one will dispute that. But we have all heard of the "good-hearted, down-to-earth bartender," who counsels his customers while they drink. Or the "prostitute with a heart of gold." Perhaps the tax collector was like that. Perhaps adversity beyond his control had put him in his base profession. Perhaps, in spite of his calling, he really loved his fellowman and put his (admittedly "ill-gotten") gains at their disposal.

We know perfectly well that is not the way this story should be taken! It is true that the Pharisee was not "justified." He was a sinner under the curse of God and God's law. But that was no less true of the tax collector. He, too, was a sinner. He, too, deserved judgment. The only difference between them was that the tax collector approached God on the basis of God's merciful acts toward sinners and not on the basis of his own supposed righteousness, while the Pharisee did not.

The clue to the meaning of this parable is the word "justified," as I indicated. But the heart of its teaching is in the tax collector's prayer: "God, have mercy on me, a sinner" (v. 13). It is one of the shortest prayers in the Bible—seven words in English, six in Greek—but it is also one of the profoundest.

Consider the beginning and end of the prayer for a moment, eliminating the middle. The words "God . . . me, a sinner" are profound, because those are the essential ingredients in all religion and because they express the essential genuine religious insight gained when a person becomes aware of God's presence. It is certainly the case—we know this in Calvin's classic expression in the *Institutes of the Christian Religion*—that the knowledge of God and the knowledge of ourselves go together. That is, we never have one without the other. To know God as the sovereign God of the universe is to know ourselves as His subjects, in rebellion against Him. To know God in His holiness is to know ourselves as sinners. To know Him as love is to see ourselves as loved though unlovely. To seek God's wisdom is to see our own foolishness in spiritual things. Since God is the only standard by which any of those things can be measured, we do not know anything properly unless we know Him. Or to put it in other terms, if we do not know God, we consider ourselves to be sovereign over our own lives, holy, loving, wise, and so on, when in reality we are none of those things.

In knowing ourselves through knowing God the matter of sin is uppermost. In any encounter with God it is His holiness, as contrasted with our sin, that most strikes the worshiper. That was the case with Adam and Eve, the first sinners. After they had sinned they deluded themselves with the idea that they were all right. They made fig-leaf aprons and went about their business. But when they heard the voice of God in the garden in the cool of the day they hid from Him among the trees (Gen. 3:8). When God asked, "Where are you?" Adam answered, "I heard you in the garden, and I was afraid because I was naked; so I hid" (vv. 9-10). Their nakedness was spiritual as well as physical, and it was their spiritual dilemma as sinners that came home to them when they heard God coming.

We find the same thing in the case of Job. Job had suffered the loss of his possessions, family, and health. When his friends came to convince him that his loss was due to some sin, either recognized or hidden, Job stoutly defended himself against their accusations. He was right to do so, for Job was suffering as an upright man — "Have you considered my servant Job? There is no one on earth like him; he is blameless and upright, a man who fears God and shuns evil" (Job 1:8). If anyone could have stood before the holiness of God, it was Job. But toward the end of the book, after God came to Job with a series of questions designed to teach something of His true majesty, Job was left nearly speechless and in a state of collapse. He replied to God, "I am unworthy—how can I reply to you? . . . Therefore I despise myself and repent in dust and ashes" (Job 40:4; 42:6).

We see the same thing in the case of Isaiah. He had received a vision of the Lord "seated on a throne, high and exalted." He heard the praise of the seraphim. But the effect on Isaiah, far from being a cause for self-satisfaction or pride that such a vision had been granted to him, was actually devastating. He responded, "Woe to me! . . . I am ruined! For I am a man of unclean lips, and I live among a people of unclean lips, and my eyes have seen the King, the LORD Almighty" (Isa. 6:5). Isaiah saw himself as ruined or undone. It was only when a coal was taken from the altar and used to purge his lips that he was able to stand upright again and respond affirmatively to God's call to him for service.

Habakkuk also had a vision of God. He had been distressed with the ungodliness in the world around him and had wondered how the ungodly could rightly triumph over the man who was more righteous. The prophet then entered his watchtower and waited for God's answer. When God did respond, Habakkuk was overcome with dread. He reported, "I heard and my heart pounded, my lips quivered at the sound; decay crept into my bones, and my legs trembled" (Hab. 3:16). Habakkuk was a prophet. But a confrontation with God, even in his case, was shattering.

Similarly, although the glory of God was veiled in the person of Jesus Christ, from time to time Christ's disciples perceived who He was, ever so slightly, and had a similar reaction. After Peter had recognized the glory of God in Christ's miracle of granting a great catch of fish in Galilee, he responded, "Go away from me, Lord; I am a sinful man!" (Luke 5:8).

When the apostle John received a revelation of Christ's glory on Patmos on the Lord's Day, seeing the risen Lord standing in the midst of the seven golden candlesticks, he "fell at his feet as though dead" and rose only after experiencing something like a resurrection (Rev. 1:17).

That is what happens when a sinner meets God, and that is how we know that the tax collector knew God (despite his reputation) while the Pharisee did not. The Pharisee began his prayer with "God." But he was not praying to God because he did not see himself as a sinner. On the other hand, the tax collector was so aware of God that "he would not even look up to heaven, but beat upon his breast and said, 'God, have mercy on me, a sinner' " (v. 13). So aware of his sin was he that he did not actually call himself "*a* sinner" at this point, though the verse is so translated, but "*the* sinner." In his own eyes he was the sinner par excellence.

MERCY-SEATED

The second remarkable thing about this prayer—and the point to which all this is leading—is that the tax collector was not only aware of his sin, deep and penetrating as that awareness was. He was also aware of what God had done to deal with his sin problem. He was a sinner, alienated from God by that sin. But God had bridged the gap, making reconciliation. Consequently, between the beginning and end of his prayer ("God" and "me, a sinner") come the words "have mercy on me." It is because of the acts of God's mercy, and only because of those acts, that this man or any other sinner can approach the Almighty.

Indeed, the prayer is even profounder than that, because, as I have indicated, it is not merely a plea for mercy—though it sounds like that in the English translation. It is a plea for mercy on the basis of what God has done.

The word translated "have mercy on" *(hilastheti)* is the verb form of the word for the "Mercy Seat" on the Ark of the Covenant in the Jewish Temple *(hilasterion)*. Therefore, it could literally (but awkwardly) be translated "be Mercy-Seated toward" or "treat me as one who comes on the basis of the blood shed on the Mercy Seat as an offering for sins."

The Ark of the Covenant was a wooden box about a yard long, covered with gold, and containing the stone tables of the law of Moses. The lid of that box was the Mercy Seat, constructed of pure gold and having on each end of it angels whose outstretched wings went backward and upward, almost meeting over the center of the Mercy Seat. Between those outstretched wings God was imagined to dwell symbolically. As it stands, the Ark is a picture of judgment intended to produce dread in the worshiper through a knowledge of his or her sin. For what does God see as He looks down from between the wings of the angels? He sees the law of Moses that we have broken. He sees that he must act toward us as Judge.

But here is where the Mercy Seat comes in, and here is why it is called the *Mercy* Seat. Upon that covering of the Ark, once a year on the Day of Atonement, the high priest sprinkled blood from an animal that had been killed moments before in the courtyard of the Temple. That animal was a substitute. It was an innocent victim dying in the place of the sinful people who deserved to die. Now, when God looks down from between the outstretched wings of the angels, He sees, not the law of Moses that we have broken, but the blood of the innocent victim. He sees that punishment has been meted out. Now His love goes out in mercy to save the one who comes to Him through faith in that sacrifice.

That is why I say that the prayer of the tax collector was so profound. Not only did it embody his faith in the way of salvation by sacrifice, it actually expressed the idea by its form. That is to say, between "God," whom we have offended, and "me, a sinner," which describes us all, comes the Mercy Seat. It is a visual as well as verbal expression of the way of salvation.

The only thing we must add is that under the Old Testament system the sacrifices were merely a picture of the only adequate sacrifice of the Lord Jesus Christ, which was yet to come. Although they were important, it was not the death of animals, however many, that actually purged away sin. The true and only atonement was that to be provided by the Lord Jesus Christ who, as the perfect Lamb of God, died in the place of sinners. When the tax collector prayed, "God, have mercy on me, a sinner," he was thinking of the animal sacrifices because, although Jesus was then present, He had not yet died. When we pray the tax collector's prayer, we think of Jesus and the way in which God has provided a full and perfect salvation through Him.

Do you think of Jesus? Have you prayed that prayer? No one will ever be justified who has not prayed it, nor will anyone be received by God who has not first of all taken his stand with sinners in need of that mercy that God alone provides.

PARABLES OF WISDOM AND FOLLY

10

FIVE FOOLISH WOMEN AND THEIR FRIENDS

(Matthew 25:1-13)

"At that time the kingdom of heaven will be like ten virgins who took their lamps and went out to meet the bridegroom. Five of them were foolish and five were wise. The foolish ones took their lamps but did not take any oil with them. The wise, however, took oil in jars along with their lamps. The bridegroom was a long time in coming, and they all became drowsy and fell asleep.

"At midnight the cry rang out: 'Here's the bridegroom! Come out to meet him!'

"Then all the virgins woke up and trimmed their lamps. The foolish ones said to the wise, 'Give us some of your oil; our lamps are going out.'

"'No,' they replied, 'there may not be enough for both us and you. Instead, go to those who sell oil and buy some for yourselves.'

"But while they were on their way to buy the oil, the bridegroom arrived. The virgins who were ready went in with him to the wedding banquet. And the door was shut.

"Later the others also came. 'Sir! Sir!' they said. 'Open the door for us!'

"But he replied, 'I tell you the truth, I don't know you.'
"Therefore keep watch, because you do not know the day
or the hour."

It is a mark of our Lord's stooping to human weakness that His
preaching often appealed to the lowest motives of His hearers. I
mean that He often appealed to base self-interest. For example,
when He was making a call to discipleship he would say. "What
good is it for a man to gain the whole world, yet forfeit his soul?"
(Mark 8:36). That statement is based on simple calculation of the
advantages and disadvantages of a course of action. We might have
preferred Him to say, "Follow Me because that is the right thing to
do" or "Follow Me because the sovereign God demands it." But
although He could have said that, He makes a different appeal: "This
is the way to save your life, which is precious to you; it is the way to
be approved in God's judgment."

In the same way He says, "Be careful not to do your 'acts of
righteousness' before men, to be seen by them. If you do, you will
have no reward from your Father in heaven" (Matt. 6:1). In this
verse the appeal for proper action is reward. Again, "If you forgive
men when they sin against you, your heavenly Father will also
forgive you. But if you do not forgive men their sins, your Father
will not forgive your sins" (Matt. 6:14-15).

There is a special category of such appeals in Christ's parables of
wisdom and folly: the five wise and five foolish virgins (Matt. 25:1-
13), the rich fool (Luke 12:16-21), a shrewd man of the world (Luke
16:1-9), and the wise and foolish builders (Luke 6:46-49). In these
stories our Lord shows that many of His hearers were foolish in
terms of their own self-interest, and He prods them to a wiser
course of action.

In the first story, the five foolish virgins miss the wedding banquet, which they had no desire to do. They wanted to attend but
they missed it, and the fault was no one's but their own. Jesus warns
His listeners against such folly. The rich fool wanted to enjoy himself. But he missed eternal happiness by a foolish preoccupation
with this world's goods. The shrewd manager was wiser in his own
way than many who profess to be God's people because he planned
for the future. The lesson of the foolish builders, who built without
a foundation, and the wise builders, who built their house on rock,

is evident. In each of these stories the Lord challenged His hearers to see life in terms of eternity and plan accordingly.

AN ESSENTIAL DIFFERENCE

The story of the ten virgins is a masterpiece, as Bible students (and others) have long recognized. It is realistic in detail and poignant in application. Besides, the deeper one explores it, the profounder are its lessons.

Jesus tells how ten young women were invited to a marriage feast. Five were wise and five were foolish. The wise women showed their wisdom by planning for the possible delay of the bridegroom. They took extra oil for their lamps so they would be ready when he came. The foolish women neglected to do so. While they waited all fell asleep. Suddenly a cry went out that the bridegroom was coming. The wise got up and trimmed their lamps. The others recognized that they were out of oil and asked to borrow some. "No," said the wise. "There may not be enough for both us and you. Instead, go to those who sell oil and buy some for yourselves." The women who were unprepared started off, but while they were gone the bridegroom came and those who were ready went in with him to the feast. The door was shut. Later the foolish virgins returned and found the door barred.

"Open the door for us!" they cried.

But the bridegroom said, "I don't know you."

The Lord concluded, "Therefore keep watch, because you do not know the day or the hour [of my return]" (Matt. 25:13).

The story is a masterpiece; it is not difficult to see its main points. Especially is that true of its chief point: the vast difference between the wise and the foolish women. In many respects they were alike. But in their preparation or lack of it they were perfect opposites. On that difference the lesson of the story turns.

It is worth seeing the ways in which the women were the same. For one thing, all ten had been invited to the banquet. There may have been many who did not receive invitations, but each of them had received one and each was therefore right in anticipating a grand occasion when the bridegroom came. Second, each had responded to the wedding invitation. Some may have disregarded it or scorned it, as the townspeople did in one of Jesus' other parables

(Matt. 22:1-14). But that was not the case with these women. They had received the invitation and had responded joyfully, which they demonstrated by waiting for the bridegroom's appearance. Third, all clearly had some affection and even love for the bridegroom. That was what had brought them to the point at which the story commences: "Ten virgins . . . took their lamps and went out to meet the bridegroom" (v. 1). Fourth, in spite of their affection, all were alike in that they became drowsy and fell asleep when the bridegroom was delayed.

But suddenly he came, and at once the similarities vanished and the essential difference emerged. Five had oil in their lamps and five did not. Five were ready and five were unprepared.

There are many in the church who fit our Lord's description—for, of course, the parable applies to the church. The setting of these last chapters of Matthew (Matt. 23-25) is the time leading up to the Lord's second coming. So we must say, on the basis of the parable as well as our own observation, that there are people within the church who have heard the invitation of Christ, have responded somewhat, and may even be said to have affection for Jesus, but who are yet not ready to meet Him. They are good church people. They would never think of speaking a word against Jesus. But they are not born again. They do not have that inward change which alone entitles them to enter heaven.

That is how the oil in the story must be taken. Some have applied it to the Holy Spirit, which is a tempting thing to do since the Holy Spirit is often symbolized by oil in Scripture. But if we do that, we start thinking that one can have the Holy Spirit and then run out of Him, as it were, or that when one runs out he needs to buy more. It is better to think of the oil simply as an inward preparation. Outwardly the women were alike. The crucial and determining difference was within.

Spurgeon obviously thought along those lines. He wrote in one of his sermons:

> A great change has to be wrought in you, far beyond any power of yours to accomplish, ere you can go in with Christ to the marriage. You must, first of all, be renewed in your nature, or you will not be ready. You must be washed from your sins, or you will not be ready. You must be justified in Christ's

righteousness, and you must put on his wedding dress, or else you will not be ready. You must be reconciled to God, you must be made like to God, or you will not be ready. Or, to come to the parable before us, you must have a lamp, and that lamp must be fed with heavenly oil, and it must continue to burn brightly, or else you will not be ready. No child of darkness can go into that place of light. You must be brought out of nature's darkness into God's marvelous light, or else you will never be ready to go in with Christ to the marriage, and to be forever with him.[1]

So the first point of the parable is a question: Are you ready? Or are you among the five foolish women who had received the invitation, responded to it, and had some form of affection for the bridegroom, but who were not inwardly prepared? You should be among the wise who, although they, too, had fallen asleep, were nevertheless ready. On that distinction hangs your soul's destiny.

A TIME OF CRISIS

The second point of the parable, which we have already hinted at, is that the difference between the condition of the wise and that of the foolish was revealed by the coming of the bridegroom. It revealed itself in crisis. During the days before the wedding or the night leading up to the start of the feast few would have noticed that five women had adequately prepared for the bridegroom's coming and five had not. But suddenly the bridegroom came, and the distinction was immediately apparent.

The same will happen when the Lord Jesus Christ returns. Many who have considered themselves true children of God will be shown not to be, and many who have perhaps not been regarded as His children will be revealed to be believers.

How are you to know whether you are in one camp or the other? To answer that question I would like to make a suggestion that is not found in the parable itself but I think flows from it. If it is true that the crisis of the Lord's return and the final judgment associated with it will bring out the real condition of those who profess Christianity, is

1. Charles Haddon Spurgeon, "Entrance and Exclusion," in *Metropolitan Tabernacle Pulpit,* vols. 7-63 (Pasadena, Tex.: Pilgrim Publications, 1976), 43:30.

it not also the case that their true condition is revealed by lesser but, nevertheless, real crisis experiences now? I believe you can preview the results of the final judgment by the way you react to crises now. Here is how one author puts it:

Nothing will more correctly reveal what is in a man than the coming upon him of some crushing and unlooked-for crisis. Let it be temporal ruin by the failure of his calculations or the disappointment of all his hopes; let it be the entrance of the death-angel into his home and the removal from it of his nearest and dearest earthly friend; let it be his own prostration by some serious illness which puts him face to face with his dissolution, and forthwith the extent of his resources is unfolded, and it is at once discovered both by others and by himself whether he is animated by unfailing faith in the Lord Jesus Christ and sustained by the grace of the Holy Spirit, or whether he has been deceiving himself, all the while relying on some other support. It was a shrewd remark of Andrew Fuller that a man has only as much religion as he can command in trial.

Let us therefore look back upon the past and analyze our experiences at such testing times as those to which I have referred. We have all had them. We have all heard already, in some form or other, this midnight cry, "Behold, the bridegroom cometh"; for in every such surprise as those which I have described, Jesus was coming to us. How did we meet him then? Did our lamps go out? Or were we able to trim them and keep them burning brightly all through? Oh, if by any such event we discovered our utter resourcelessness, let us betake ourselves now to Christ that he may thoroughly renew us by his Holy Spirit and so prepare us for that last and solemnest crisis when over the graves of the slumbering dead the archangel shall cry out, "Behold, the bridegroom cometh," and all shall arise to stand before his great white throne.[2]

THREE MORE LESSONS

This parable has three more lessons that I want to treat briefly.

2. William M. Taylor, *The Parables of Our Saviour Expounded and Illustrated* (New York: A. C. Armstrong and Son, 1900), pp. 170-71.

First, *the life of the Lord Jesus Christ within is not transferable.* I do not mean by that that one saved person may not be used of God to bring the gospel to another, for that happens, of course. Paul speaks of the gospel being passed "from faith to faith" (Rom. 1:17, KJV). I mean that no person can get by on another's faith. You cannot be saved by the life of Christ in another.

Many people delude themselves along those lines. They do not have true faith in Christ, but they have been exposed to it over a period of years and suppose that in the time of Christ's judgment they will be able to appeal to God's work in the life of someone close to them.

"What right do you have to come into My heaven?"

"Well, I don't really know how to answer that, Lord. But I call your attention to my mother. She was a godly woman, and I learned a lot from her."

"I didn't ask that," the Lord replies. "I asked: What right do *you* have to enter My heaven?"

"Look at my Sunday school teachers, Lord! They were godly people; they certainly went out of their way to teach me. They prayed for me, too. Don't forget them!"

Jesus replies, "What right do *you* have to enter heaven?"

I make the point because I believe it is the proper understanding of the five wise women refusing to give their oil to the five foolish ones. As a literal story, that seems uncharitable. The selfless thing for the wise women to do would have been for them to share their oil, even if it meant that they themselves would have run out. But the story is not moving on that level. It is teaching spiritual things, and in particular, that in the day of Christ's coming each person must stand on his own. Your mother's faith will not save you. Your wife's faith will not be useful to you. You will not be saved by the spiritual life of your son or daughter. The question will be: Where do *you* stand? Are *you* alive in Christ? Are *you* ready?

Second, *lost opportunities cannot be regained.* The foolish women set out to buy oil. But the bridegroom was coming then, and they already were too late. The time to have bought oil was past. So will it be when Christ returns to judgment! Those who are ready will be taken in to the marriage feast, and those who are not ready will be shut out.

Are you unsaved? If so, this moment is your opportunity. Do not say, "I will turn to Christ later. I will repent after I enjoy a few more years of sin. There is always time for Jesus." You do not know that. Today may be the last time you will hear the gospel. Even if it is not — even if you do hear it again and again — it will be no easier for you to turn to God later. In fact, the opposite is the case. The fact that you have rejected the free offer of God's grace now will harden you so that you will find it much more difficult to repent later. God may break you: He may do it through suffering, misery, or frustration. But He may not, and wisdom tells you to prepare now. "I tell you, now is the time of God's favor, now is the day of salvation" (2 Cor. 6:2).

Third, *the Lord always comes without warning.* He will do it in the day of His second coming. That is why the parable ends with the words: "Therefore keep watch, because you do not know the day or the hour" (v. 13). Jesus will also come without warning on the day of your death, which amounts to the same thing.

As I prepared this study, I called a pastor who had been a friend of mine in seminary. He had come from Wyoming and after seminary had gone back to pastor a church in the small valley where he had grown up. I was calling him because he had called me several weeks before, seeking advice about some trouble he was having in his church. A woman answered the phone — it turned out to be his mother — and told me that my friend, her son, was dead. He had suffered a sudden and unexpected stroke just two weeks before, lingered for ten days, and then had died. He was a believer. But death had come suddenly, and he was in the presence of his Lord.

Is Jesus your Lord? Make sure of it, if you are uncertain. And "keep watch, because you do not know the day or the hour" in which you will be called to meet Him.

11

THE RICH FOOL

(Luke 12:13-21)

Someone in the crowd said to him, "Teacher, tell my brother to divide the inheritance with me."

Jesus replied, "Man, who appointed me a judge or an arbiter between you?" Then he said to them, "Watch out! Be on your guard against all kinds of greed; a man's life does not consist in the abundance of his possessions."

And he told them this parable: "The ground of a certain rich man produced a good crop. He thought to himself, 'What shall I do? I have no place to store my crops.'

"Then he said, 'This is what I'll do. I will tear down my barns and build bigger ones, and there I will store my grain and my goods. And I'll say to myself, "You have plenty of good things laid up for many years. Take life easy; eat, drink and be merry."'

"But God said to him, 'You fool! This very night your life will be demanded from you. Then who will get what you have prepared for yourself?'

"This is how it will be with anyone who stores up things for himself but is not rich toward God."

The second of the Lord's parables of wisdom and folly is the story of the rich fool. Unlike the previous parable, it does not present a contrast between one who was wise and one who was foolish. It is entirely about folly, the folly of being preoccupied with riches. The emphasis on wisdom comes out only at the last, when the Lord tells

His listeners to be "rich," not in this world's things but "toward God." The story has a setting. On this occasion, as Jesus was teaching, someone rudely interrupted to say that his brother had refused to divide an inheritance with him and to ask Jesus to tell his brother to share it. The demand was entirely out of line, as Jesus immediately pointed out. He was not a judge in Israel. There were courts to settle such things. But rather than let the incident drop, Jesus went on to warn against an attitude that would be so preoccupied with material possessions it would exclude spiritual concerns. "Watch out!" [He said.] "Be on your guard against all kinds of greed; a man's life does not consist in the abundance of his possessions" (v. 15).

That statement is ample in itself for long, serious meditation, particularly by people living in our modern culture where the opposite is apparently true. We measure the worth of an individual largely in terms of his possessions. But the Lord did not stop at that point. He went on to tell of a rich fool. According to the story, a man had an abundant crop one year, so large that he did not have room to store it. He could have distributed the surplus to the poor—that may be what Jesus is suggesting—but he did not. Instead he said, "I will tear down my barns and build bigger ones, and there I will store all my grain and my goods. And I'll say to myself, 'You have plenty of good things laid up for many years. Take life easy; eat, drink, and be merry' " (vv. 18-19). That was worldly wisdom, the kind many people practice today. But Jesus said that God regarded that as the height of folly. "But God said to him, 'You fool! This very night your life will be demanded from you. Then who will get what you have prepared for yourself?' " (v. 20).

The Lord concluded, "This is how it will be with anyone who stores up things for himself but is not rich toward God" (v. 21).

MISUSE OF WEALTH

There are not many places in the Bible where God calls people fools, so the fact that He singles out a preoccupation with things as folly is striking. In the Old Testament the man who says there is no God, that is, the atheist, is called a fool (Ps. 14:1; 53:1). So if that rich materialist is called a fool, it puts him right up there in the company of the God-deniers. In fact, there is an obvious connection, for regardless of his intellectual opinions, the man who operates like the fool of Christ's parable is a practical atheist after all.

Why was that man foolish? There are a number of reasons. First, he misused the wealth God had given. He would probably have denied that it was God who had given him the wealth. He had plowed the fields, planted the grain, tended the soil, and gathered the harvest. He had done it himself. The wealth was his, and he had no responsibility to anyone. But that is not the way Jesus viewed the matter. Jesus did not say, "A certain man worked very hard and accumulated a great fortune." He said, "The ground of a certain rich man produced a good crop" (v. 16). Jesus undoubtedly meant that the man's prosperity was from God, who made the ground and prospered the harvest. The man had worked, true. But apart from the blessing of God he might have suffered blight or drought and thus have had no harvest at all. The rich man's blessing was from God, but he failed to see that. He regarded the wealth as his rather than God's, and therefore misused it. He thought it was all for him, so he stored it up, taking no thought of anyone else.

We need to say something else at this point. That man misused his wealth by failing to see that it had come to him from God. That was a bad mistake. But it is a common one, since there is a tendency for wealth to produce just such a distortion. Wealth tends to trap us into self-absorption, materialism, and insensitivity to others—just as sin traps us. If that were not the case, why would Jesus have said, "It is easier for a camel to go through the eye of a needle than for a rich man to enter the kingdom of God" (Matt. 19:24)?

The Bible is not against possessions when they are properly used; we are going to come back to that point. But we must not allow the truth that riches can be properly used to blind us to the fact that they are generally misused, or to the fact that they may ruin our own spirituality. Many biblical examples of wrongly acquired or misused wealth should alert us to the danger. In the book of Joshua we are told of the sin of Achan that caused the defeat of the armies of Israel at Ai. Israel had been victorious at Jericho and had dedicated the spoil of the battle to God, as God intended. But there was a blemish on the victory. During the battle Achan had come upon a Babylonian garment, two hundred pieces of silver, and an ingot of gold. Because he coveted them he hid them in his tent. It was a small thing, but it was disobedience to God and caused Israel to be defeated in its next engagement (Josh. 7).

Solomon allowed the love of affluence to ruin his life. Ananias and Sapphira lied to the Lord about money, pretending that they had given the full price of a sale to the church while actually keeping back a portion. They were struck dead (Acts 5). Paul wrote in one of his letters about a man named Demas, who "because he loved this world has deserted me . . ." (2 Tim. 4:10).

We see the same thing today when people put a home and the care of it above the need for Bible teaching and will thus mow the grass on Sunday when they should be at church. Or men will direct their efforts toward amassing a fortune (or part of one) while neglecting their families and the essential spiritual life of their home. No wonder Paul told Timothy, "The love of money is a root of all kinds of evil" (1 Tim. 6:10).

The Bible does not teach that money is evil in itself or that things in themselves produce evil. The fault is in those who use it. Before God created Adam and Eve He created a vast world of pleasant and useful things for them. They were meant for our use in every joyful and constructive way. But when man sinned the things that were to be helpful to him usurped God's place in his heart. So he began to fight, steal, cheat, and do countless other things to possess them. Today, when a person surrenders to God and allows Him to redirect his life, a process begins in which things are removed from the center and God is again reinstated on the throne.

There have been sensitive souls in the history of the church who have recognized the evils that accompany possessions and who have sought to eliminate the evils by doing away with the possessions. Using the example of the early church in Jerusalem, which for a time pooled its possessions and distributed to those who had need, these Christians argue against the right of private property and at times even advocate a form of Christian communism. That is not right. If some Christians are led of the Lord to sell their possessions and give to others, particularly in a time of need, that is a great blessing. But it does not follow that all Christians should copy their example.

Far from condemning the possession of private property the Bible actually assumes the rightness of it. For instance, the eighth commandment says, "You shall not steal" (Exod. 20:15). That teaches that I am not to take things that belong to another person, and neither is he to take mine. In the story of Ananias and Sapphira mentioned above, Peter said, when speaking to the husband, "Ananias, how is it that Satan has so filled your heart that you have lied to the Holy Spirit and have kept for yourself some of the money you received for the land? Didn't it belong to you before it was sold? And after it was sold, wasn't the money at your disposal? What made you think of doing such a thing? You have not lied to men but to God" (Acts 5:3-4). In that statement, although Peter is exposing Ananias's hypocrisy, he, nevertheless, indirectly recognizes the right of private property and states that God does not require anyone to dispose of it.

If someone asks, "But didn't the Lord instruct the rich young ruler to sell what he had and give to the poor?" the answer is that He did not say it to Mary or Martha or Lazarus or John the Evangelist or Zebedee. He said it to the *rich young ruler,* whose chief obstruction to a life of following Christ lay in his possessions (which he proved by turning away). For such a person—and there are many today—the surrender of possessions would be the most significant blessing of their lives. Giving their goods away would be even better. That does not mean, however, that possessions in themselves are wrong or, for that matter, that poverty is a particularly blessed form of Christianity.

No, in that area of the Christian life the true solution does not lie in the accumulation or renunciation of wealth. It lies in the proper use and proper estimate of the things God has provided. In other words, we are not called to relinquish things but to use them under God's direction for the health and well-being of ourselves and our families, for material aid to others and for promoting God's truth.

POSSESSIONS WILL PERISH

Misuse of his wealth was not the only reason God called the rich man foolish, however. In fact, it is not even the chief reason. The chief reason the man was foolish is that he allowed his concern for riches to eclipse the far more important concern that he should have had for his soul. That was bad business even from a worldly standpoint, because possessions are perishable goods while the soul is intended to dwell with God forever.

I said as I began the parables of wisdom and folly that our Lord characteristically appealed to self-interest. I think, however, that of all such appeals there is none that presents the issue on such a low level as does this parable. Think of it. It is the story of a dying man, a man leaving this world to spend an eternity in hell without God. In

108 • The Parables of Jesus

such circumstances Jesus could well have argued, "Consider what you have gained in terms of what you are losing. Compare your present pleasures with your future deprivation and suffering." He could have said, "Weigh the value of your soul over against your possessions." But that is not what He said. He knew the man had no regard for such things. He did not value his soul. So the Lord comes down to the level on which he is operating and talks about his possessions only. His argument is, "You fool! This very night your life will be demanded from you. *Then who will get what you have prepared for yourself?*" The one thing that might possibly get through to such a man was the thought of someone else enjoying what he had spent his life to gain. Think of that, if nothing else will move you. The Spanish have a grim proverb: "There are no pockets in a shroud."

One man met another in a streetcar one day, and they began to talk about a millionnaire whose death had been announced that morning in the paper. "How much did he leave?" one asked.

"All he had," the other answered.

Everything you have must one day be left behind. It is yours now to use or abuse, but one day it will be taken from you and you will stand naked before Him who is your maker. How will you stand in that day? Will you stand as one who has put God first and has therefore come to see possessions as a gift from Him to be used for God's work? Or will you be one of many who have sold out to possessions, to the exclusion of all else, and have died without hope of salvation?

RICH TOWARD GOD

In the last three words of the parable Jesus gives a clue to what the goal of the wise man should be. He should be "rich toward God," Jesus says (v. 21). A phrase like that could be elaborated at great length, but its basic meaning is quite obvious. It means that one is to be rich in spiritual things, which will last, as opposed to being rich only in material things, which will not last. One spiritual treasure is faith. James says, "Has not God chosen those who are poor in the eyes of the world to be rich in faith and to inherit the kingdom he promised those who love him?" (James 2:5). Another treasure is good deeds. Paul told Timothy to instruct those under his care "to be rich in good deeds, and to be generous and willing to share. In this way they will lay up treasure for themselves as a firm foundation for the coming age" (1 Tim. 6:18-19). The opposite is those who build a life of "wood, hay or straw" and who are saved, if they are saved, "only as . . . escaping through the flames" (1 Cor. 3:12, 15).

One writer says, "Faith in Jesus Christ enriches us by giving us the blessings of forgiveness, peace, holiness and heaven; and good works, wrought as the outcome of gratitude for these blessings, enrich us with present happiness and future reward. These are things which the world cannot give or take away. These are things which are the possessions of our soul, and of which death cannot deprive us."[1]

What must we do to achieve such riches? There are two prerequisites. First, we must determine that we really want them and that we, therefore, are willing to serve God first and foremost, rather than our possessions. The Lord Himself said, "You cannot serve both God and Money" (Matt. 6:24). The word translated here as "money" is the Hebrew word *mammon,* meaning "material possessions." It came from a root meaning "to entrust" or "to place in someone's keeping." Mammon, therefore, meant "the wealth entrusted to another."

At that period of its development the word did not have any bad connotations. A rabbi could say, "Let the mammon of thy neighbor be as dear to thee as thine own." When a bad sense was meant, an adjective or some other qualifying word was added, as in "the mammon of unrighteousness" or "unrighteous mammon." As time passed, however, the meaning of the word shifted away from the passive mood ("that which is entrusted") to the active ("that in which one trusts"). Now the word, whose original meaning was best represented by a small *m,* came to be spelled with a capital letter as designating a god.

That development repeats itself in anyone who does not have his eyes fixed on spiritual treasures. Have things become your god? Do they obscure God? It may not be so, but if you think more about your home, car, vacation, bank account, clothes, makeup, or investments than God, then you are serving Mammon and building treasure on earth. According to Jesus, "Where your treasure is, there your heart will be also" (Matt. 6:21).

1. William M. Taylor, *The Parables of Our Saviour Expounded and Illustrated* (New York: A. C. Armstrong and Son, 1900), pp. 274-75.

The second necessary thing if we are to become rich toward God is that we must empty ourselves of anything that would take the place of those spiritual riches. We must become poor in spirit before we can become rich in spiritual blessings (Matt. 5:3). We must empty the heart of greed, pride, and other sins so that the riches of God can flow in.

That is what God's children have found. Before his conversion Augustine was proud of his intellect and knowledge, and his pride kept him from believing on Christ. It was only after he had emptied himself of his pride and the sense of being able to manage his own life perfectly that he found God's wisdom through the Bible. Martin Luther's experience was similar. When the future reformer entered the monastery at a young age it was to earn his salvation through piety and good works. Nevertheless, he had an acute sense of failure. It was only after he had recognized his own inability to please God and had emptied himself of all attempts to earn salvation that God touched his heart and showed him the true way. A hymn writer has written:

> But tho' I cannot sing, or tell, or know
> The fullness of Thy love, while here below,
> My empty vessel I may freely bring:
> O Thou, who art of love the living spring,
> My vessel fill.

> I am an empty vessel—not one thought
> Or look of love, I ever to Thee brought;
> Yet I may come, and come again to Thee,
> With this, the empty sinner's only plea—
> Thou lovest me*

An empty vessel! That is what you must be if God is to fill you with the life of Christ and enable you to live for Him—even in the use of your possessions.

---

*Source unknown.

12

A SHREWD MAN OF THE WORLD

(Luke 16:1-9)

Jesus told his disciples: "There was a rich man whose manager was accused of wasting his possessions. So he called him in and asked him, 'What is this I hear about you? Give an account of your management, because you cannot be manager any longer.'

"The manager said to himself, 'What shall I do now? My master is taking away my job. I'm not strong enough to dig, and I'm ashamed to beg—I know what I'll do so that, when I lose my job here, people will welcome me into their houses.'

"So he called in each one of his master's debtors. He asked the first, 'How much do you owe my master?'

" 'Eight hundred gallons of olive oil,' he replied.

"The manager told him, 'Take your bill, sit down quickly, and make it four hundred.'

"Then he asked the second, 'And how much do you owe?'

" 'A thousand bushels of wheat,' he replied.

"He told him, 'Take your bill and make it eight hundred.'

"The master commended the dishonest manager because he had acted shrewdly. For the people of this world are more shrewd in dealing with their own kind than are the people of the light. I tell you, use worldly wealth to gain friends for yourselves, so that when it is gone, you will be welcomed into eternal dwellings."

Sin traps people in indifference so that they often become more foolish about their self-preservation than animals. Geese and other birds will fly south as winter approaches. Rodents will store up for winter. Some animals hibernate. But human beings proceed in a manner they know is foolish and characteristically fail to make adequate provision for their future.

There are some exceptions to that, however, and one of Christ's parables concerns just such an individual. He was an estate manager for a rich man, the kind of manager Eliezer might have been for Abraham, or Joseph for Potiphar. It is said of Potiphar that "he left in Joseph's care everything he had; with Joseph in charge, he did not concern himself with anything except the food he ate" (Gen. 39:6). The man in Christ's story had that kind of authority. But unlike Joseph or Eliezer, who were models of integrity, this man was dishonest. He cheated his master, and the story begins with the revelation of his dishonesty. The master called him in and asked him, "What is this I hear about you? Give an account of your management, because you cannot be manager any longer" (Luke 16:2).

The steward was faced with a crisis. What was he to do? He took stock of the situation and concluded that he did not have the strength to do manual work and that he was too proud to beg. So he fixed on a plan in which he reduced the debt of all those who owed his master anything. One debtor owed eight hundred gallons of olive oil. He reduced it to four hundred. Another owed a thousand bushels of wheat. He made it eight hundred. He assumed that by doing that he would so endear himself to his master's debtors or even implicate them in his dishonesty that when he lost his job, as he was sure to do, they would welcome him into their homes.

Jesus then said, "The master commended the dishonest manager because he had acted shrewdly. For the people of this world are more shrewd in dealing with their own kind than are the people of the light. I tell you, use worldly wealth to gain friends for yourselves, so that when it is gone, you will be welcomed into eternal dwellings" (vv. 8-9).

CLEAR THINKING

This parable has been a problem for many readers because they have imagined that our Lord is commending dishonesty. But of course, that is not what Jesus is doing. Even in the story, it is not the Lord who utters words of commendation but "the master," and even then the praise is only for the dishonest man's shrewdness. There is only one way the manager is set before us as an example, and that is in his ability to see what was coming and plan for it. In that one characteristic—though he was certainly far from commendable in other ways—he was eminently wiser than countless people who perhaps have never cheated anyone out of anything yet fail to plan for that moment when they must, each one, give an accounting before God.

When we analyze the shrewdness the manager showed, we find it in four areas. In each he is a model for the foolish of this world.

First, the manager *saw the issues clearly.* We can imagine a situation in which a person might try to wish away his problem. He had been discovered and was now required to give an accounting. He had been threatened with the loss of his job. He could have thought: "It's true that I'm in a fix and will have a hard time getting out of it. But I've been in difficult places before and have always squeaked through. Perhaps my master will not be able to detect the tampering I've done with his books. Or, even if he does, he may feel sorry for me and keep me on after all." Again, the manager might have been so paralyzed at the thought of appearing before his master, books in hand, that he would have refused to think about his problem at all. He might have tried to wish it away. But that was not the case. When confronted by his master he knew at once that the "jig" was up. He could not disguise his dishonesty, and the only thing left was to plan for the future as best he could.

If the Lord were spelling out the points of the parable He might say at that juncture, "It would be good if all people could see the issues as clearly as that dishonest steward could. You are all stewards of what God has entrusted to you. You are wasting His possessions. One day you must give an accounting. Think how it will stand with you in that day and prepare for it."

One thing that appalls me about so many people today is the muddle-headed thinking on ultimate issues they willingly foster and accept. It is part of the relativism of our age that many are quite willing to have several mutually contradictory notions on any subject floating around in their heads at any one time, and never seem to feel it wise or even eventually necessary to sort those things out. According to such people, there may be a God. But again, there may not be. If He exists, He may be personal or He may not be. He may have revealed Himself or He may not have.

Jesus may be the supreme revelation of this God. Or again, some other religious figure may be a supreme revelation. Jesus' death may have been necessary, or it may not have been. Faith in Jesus may be the way of salvation, or it may not be. There may be a heaven, but there are also good reasons why there probably is not. People who permit such confusion are not simply undecided; they are contradictory in their actions. That is, sometimes they operate as if there is a God who has revealed Himself in Jesus Christ. But at other times they act as if He does not exist or, if He does, that His existence is one of the most insignificant facts of their experience.

That is what is really incredible—that people can operate in such a contradictory fashion. If you are doing that, I challenge you to learn from the dishonest manager and think clearly. Think along these lines:

1. If there is no God, then I am a law to myself and can do as I please. But of course, life then has no more meaning than I can give to it, and there is nothing beyond. If there is a God, then I am made by Him and owe Him a corresponding allegiance and worship. My problem begins with the realization that I have not done that and must therefore be the object of His great displeasure.

2. If there is a God, that God has either revealed Himself or He has not. If He has not, I am back in the same place as if there was no God, for all practical purposes. On the other hand, if God has revealed Himself (as we have every right to expect He would do), then it is my duty to seek out that revelation and make my way to Him. My problem is compounded by that duty because I have *not* sought Him. On the contrary, I have run from Him and have tried every means to banish His presence and influence from my life.

3. Jesus may be just another religious teacher. If so, His

teachings can be used or not, as they prove helpful or unhelpful. But if He is more than a religious teacher, if He is God come in human flesh, as He claimed, then His teachings demand more than just a casual perusal. They demand belief and obedience. I am in trouble here because I have not believed in Him or obeyed Him.

4. If Jesus is not God, then His death and His teachings about its meaning are unimportant, though they were obviously important to Him. But if He is God, then His death is of the utmost importance. He taught—and He must be believed if He is God—that no one will ever be saved who does not believe that He died in his place to satisfy the just wrath of God against the sinner. That means that if I have not believed in Jesus as my Savior, I am doomed to suffer for my own sins when I eventually appear before God to give an accounting of all I have done or failed to do.

5. If there is a heaven and a hell, it is only common sense and enlightened self-interest for me to do everything I can do to gain the former and avoid the latter.

Is it not possible to think clearly in such matters? Can you not sort out the issues, reach your conclusions, and then act? Do not muddle along any longer with your head in the clouds and your feet in both God's and the devil's camps. God Himself challenges you to such clear thinking. It was just such a challenge that God gave the Israelites when they were trying to worship both Jehovah and Baal. Elijah built an altar on Mount Carmel and challenged the priests of Baal to do the same. After the altars were built the sacrifices were added. Everything was there but fire, and the true God—Jehovah or Baal—was to provide it. Jehovah answered by fire so great that not merely the sacrifice, but the wood, stones, soil, and water were consumed by it. That was after Elijah had uttered the great challenge: "How long will you waver between two opinions? If the LORD is God, follow him; but if Baal is God, follow him" (1 Kings 18:21).

That is the challenge presented to you today. Do not waver between two opinions. Think it through. If God is God, serve Him. But if not, then follow a Baal of your choosing and discover the end that he has prepared for his disciples.

CONCERN FOR ONE'S SOUL

The second area in which the dishonest manager is commended to us for his shrewdness is in his *care for the future*. We can imagine a case in which a man of his stripe might perceive quite clearly what the outcome of his dishonest career was to be. He would not delude himself with thinking that the master would forgive him or that he could bluff his way through the crisis. He would know that the game was up. But he might not care. With a certain "So what?" attitude he might say, "Let come what may. I've had my fun. It's been great while it lasted. I'm going to face whatever happens with a shrug." That was not his approach. He did care what happened, and as a result he made rapid provision for the outcome.

Have you ever talked to an insurance agent? If you have not, your first conversation can be overwhelming in the sense that you would never have believed the kinds of things you can be (and according to the agent, should be) insured for. Most of us know about life insurance—but there are several kinds of that. There is also disability insurance, health insurance, dental insurance, car insurance (in several categories), home owners' insurance (fire, theft, casualty), mortgage insurance, and other varieties. Since the insurance companies are still in business and seem to be thriving, many people are presumably insuring themselves against all kinds of calamities—the majority of which will never happen. But they do not care enough about their souls to insure themselves against the one thing that most certainly will happen: they must die, meet God, and give an accounting.

Think back to the preceding parable in which God says to the rich farmer, "You fool! This very night your life will be demanded from you. Then who will get what you have prepared for yourself?" (Luke 12:20).

PREPARE TO MEET GOD

The dishonest manager is also an example for us because *he made provision for what he knew was coming*. That is, he not only saw the issues clearly and cared about the outcome, he also did something about it. In spiritual terms we would say that, according to his example, the one who has been awakened to the fact that he must meet God and who knows himself to be unprepared for the encounter should bend every effort to get ready. He should seek out Christian teaching, learn what God has done for his salvation, and then believe on the Lord Jesus Christ as his Savior—for salvation rests on what Jesus has done.

It is interesting, however, that in this context Jesus emphasizes not so much faith in His own person as He does a proper use of money, which we tend to think of as being unimportant or at least not a spiritual concern. This parable follows that of the prodigal son, which ends with the older brother's unbalanced concern for property ("This son of yours . . . has squandered your property with prostitutes"). It also comes before the parable of the rich man and Lazarus. In this life the rich man had "good things" but used them on himself and thus squandered them, while Lazarus had nothing. In heaven the tables are reversed. Even more important, the parable of the shrewd manager ends with an application to money and is followed by a discussion of the uses of wealth. Jesus says,

"I tell you, use worldly wealth to gain friends for yourselves, so that when it is gone, you will be welcomed into eternal dwellings.

"Whoever can be trusted with very little can also be trusted with much, and whoever is dishonest with very little will also be dishonest with much. So if you have not been trustworthy in handling worldly wealth, who will trust you with true riches? And if you have not been trustworthy with someone else's property, who will give you property of your own?

"No servant can serve two masters. Either he will hate the one and love the other, or he will be devoted to the one and despise the other. You cannot serve both God and Money." [Luke 16:9-13]

Those statements do not seem to be in any logical order, but are rather aphorisms growing out of the parable about money. They make three points. First, the Lord says to use money to make friends who will precede us to heaven, so that when the money is gone, as it certainly will be one day, the friends will remain. It is not a case (the reader will understand this) of buying friends in heaven, above all of buying God's favor. Rather it is similar to that of the sheep and the goats found in Matthew 25. In that story the righteous used their possessions to feed the hungry, give drink to those who were thirsty, clothe the naked, welcome strangers, and visit the sick and imprisoned. The Lord showed that to be a proper use of wealth. The wicked did none of those things.

Second, the Lord makes a point about trust, showing that a person must prove faithful in little things before being trusted with large things. There seem to be expanding areas of trust: 1. small units of other people's wealth, 2. large units of other people's wealth, 3. one's own wealth, and 4. spiritual wealth. There is a suggestion here of another of Christ's parables in which a servant entrusted with five talents used them wisely and was entrusted with five more, a man entrusted with two talents used them wisely and was entrusted with two more, but a servant who was given one talent did not use it and had even that one talent taken away (Matt. 25:14-30; cf. Luke 19:11-27). Clearly the Lord Jesus takes such matters seriously. How we handle our money is a tip-off to how faithful we would be in other areas, and faithfulness in this and all areas of earthly responsibility is rewarded with spiritual treasures.

Third, the Lord flatly declares that a person cannot serve both God and money. Many try, or pretend to, but it cannot be done. Either God is Lord and, therefore, He determines how our wealth and other possessions are to be used, or money is lord, and *it* will determine what place (if any) we have for God and His concerns.

The shrewd manager of Christ's parable should be emulated in one final point; *he moved quickly*. Having seen the issues clearly and caring deeply for his future, he made provision at once. He did not delay; there was no time to lose. Neither is there time for you to lose if you are not yet in a right relationship to God.

Professor John Gerstner tells of a time when he and his wife were in Kashmir and were returning home in a little boat that had just pulled up alongside a bigger junk by the shore. As they were sitting there another boat went by and some water splashed on them. The houseboat owner became very excited and gestured that they should get out. Gerstner, utterly unmoved, said to his wife, "See how excitable these people are! We get slightly damp, and you would think it was a catastrophe."

The man kept gesturing furiously. Gerstner replied, "It's OK, Kuzra; it's OK."

At last the owner became so disturbed that he broke out of his dialect, which they had not been able to understand, and shouted,

"No OK!" The American couple got the message and quickly climbed out of the junk. The owner then tossed his grandchild to them and jumped out himself, and when they turned around, the boat they had been in was gone. The undertow had swallowed it up. If they had delayed a moment longer, they would have been taken under with it.

That is the message; you are not OK! The sooner you see that, the sooner you will turn from your own efforts at salvation to the provision that God Himself has made in Jesus Christ, and you will jump from certain destruction into His strong arms.

13

WISE AND FOOLISH BUILDERS

(Luke 6:46-49)

"Why do you call me, 'Lord, Lord,' and do not do what I say? I will show what he is like who comes to me and hears my words and puts them into practice. He is like a man building a house, who dug down deep and laid the foundation on rock. When a flood came, the torrent struck that house but could not shake it, because it was well built. But the one who hears my words and does not put them into practice is like a man who built a house on the ground without a foundation. The moment the torrent struck that house, it collapsed and its destruction was complete."

I have never met anyone who built a structure of lasting worth without a foundation, and I suppose that is only natural since to do that would be the height of folly. Yet it is strange (since that is so) that so many people build their spiritual lives without foundations and are therefore carried away by the first strong winds of adversity.

Our Lord must have seen many such people in His day, even among those who were apparently quite religious. They followed Him around, listening to His teachings, and when they addressed Him they said, "Lord, Lord. . . ." But they did not do what He said, and for that fatal failure Jesus compared them to people who were building without a foundation.

In a similar passage at the end of the Sermon on the Mount, Jesus said, "Everyone who hears these words of mine and does not put them into practice is like a foolish man who built his house on sand. The rain came down, the streams rose, and the winds blew and beat against that house, and it fell with a great crash" (Matt. 7:26-27).

It is important to see that those words were not spoken of people who rebelled against Christ's teachings at all, but to people who listened to them and made profession of faith. Their folly is of a different order than that of mere unbelievers. It is the folly of people who have heard what is right, have acknowledged that it is right, and profess to be following it, but who do not put Christ's teachings into practice.

THE FOOLISH BUILDER

We need to think about those foundationless builders. We need to begin by realizing that on the surface everything seems to be quite well with them. They profess all the right things. They associate with true believers. As long as life goes smoothly it is difficult to distinguish them from the wise who have built on a firm foundation.

Toward the end of one summer, after having spent several months in Europe, I had the opportunity of returning to the United States on a student ship that sailed to New York City from Rotterdam. As I boarded that particular ship I thought that it was probably the smallest ship allowed on the ocean. Later I discovered that it was slow and very light in high seas. We boarded one afternoon and set sail at dusk. By the next morning we were still in the English Channel—within sight of Holland, I supposed. Several days later we were in sight of Land's End, England. The crossing took nine days. We had difficulty with the weather. It was the hurricane season, and a number of storms were churning up the ocean. We arrived in New York after more than a week of tossing about like a cork in a bathtub, and we experienced our first real calm as we entered the harbor.

It was quite an experience. We arrived at night, but because I did not want to miss it I stayed on deck until the early hours of the morning. I watched the ship maneuver into place in the channel, drop anchor, and stop. Then I saw the gray spires of lower Manhattan and later the rest of the New York skyline emerge like mountains in the brightening dawn. I thought of how firm they appeared and of the contrast between those anchored buildings and my own unanchored life during the previous nine days.

During still another summer my family and I made a trip that took us from Bellinzona, Switzerland, to Milan, Italy, and then on toward Venice by train as darkness fell over the great Po valley of northern Italy. We had a magnificent journey, including a sumptuous dinner, and then arrived in Venice about 12:30 P.M. As we motored down the Grand Canal under the warm Italian sky to the Piazza San Marco, where our hotel was located, I remember having quite a different impression from when I had sailed into New York. Venice is somewhat like New York. They are both great ports, and financial centers. They boast impressive buildings. But I knew, even as I gazed at the great Venetian buildings, that Venice was slowly sinking into the waters of the Adriatic Sea. The difference was that Venice has no foundations.

Many people are like that. Their lives present a magnificent display, which is sometimes the object of admiration of other people. But they do not have the foundation of the practice of Christ's teaching. Spurgeon spoke of talk without practice as temptation: "The common temptation is, instead of really repenting, to *talk about* repentance; instead of heartily believing, to *say,* 'I believe,' without believing; instead of truly loving, to *talk* of love without loving; instead of coming to Christ, to *speak* about coming to Christ, and *profess* to come to Christ, and yet not to come at all."[1]

Does a description like that fit your "Christianity"? If so, you should take Christ's parable of the wise and foolish builders as a warning and give attention to your life's foundations. You should dig deeply and not cease working until you are anchored in the Lord's teachings.

THE WISE BUILDER

In contrast to the foolish man who built his house on the sand, the Lord also speaks of a wise man who built on rock. In the Sermon on the Mount the Lord says of such a man, "The rain came down, the streams rose, and the winds blew and beat against that house; yet it did not fall, because it had its foundation on the rock" (Matt. 7:25).

What does it mean to build your house on the rock or to dig deeply and lay a foundation? In each of those versions of the parable Jesus is talking about His teaching, but that does not mean simply that we are

1. Charles Haddon Spurgeon, "On Laying Foundations," in *Metropolitan Tabernacle Pulpit,* vols. 28-37 (London: Banner of Truth, 1971), 29:51.

to go out and try to be a bit more moral, even if the morality we seek to practice is Christ's. That is involved, as we shall see. But it is more; it is a matter of building on Jesus Himself, if only because so many of Jesus' teachings were about Himself. Clearly, to practice His words means, in the first instance, to believe that He is who He says He is and to turn from sin to faith in Him as the way of salvation. Moreover, that is the most important meaning of the word "rock" or "foundation" in Scripture. Characteristically, God or His Anointed One, the Messiah, is the rock.

Not all Bible passages use the image in that way, of course. In 1 Timothy 6:17-19, Paul speaks of good works as a foundation: "Command those who are rich in this present world . . . to do good. . . . In this way they will lay up treasure for themselves as a firm foundation for the coming age." Paul also speaks of God's eternal decree in election as our foundation: "Nevertheless, God's solid foundation stands firm, sealed with this inscription: 'The Lord knows those who are his' " (2 Tim. 2:19). But those are exceptions, because for each one of such texts there are many more that apply the same imagery to Jesus Himself or to the Father.

Isaiah writes, "This is what the Sovereign LORD says: 'See, I lay a stone in Zion, a tested stone, a precious cornerstone for a sure foundation' " (Isa. 28:16). Paul declares, "You are . . . built on the foundation of the apostles and prophets, with Christ Jesus himself as the chief cornerstone" (Eph. 2:19-20). Shortly after the resurrection Peter told the Sanhedrin, "He [Jesus] is 'the stone you builders rejected, which has become the capstone' " (Acts 4:11). He wrote in his first letter, " 'See, I lay a stone in Zion, a chosen and precious cornerstone, and the one who trusts in him will never be put to shame.' Now to you who believe, this stone is precious. But to those who do not believe, 'The stone the builders rejected has become the capstone' " (1 Pet. 2:6-7). That is the true sense of Christ's teaching: "If you want a life that will last for eternity, build on Me." We sing:

> My hope is built on nothing less
> Than Jesus' blood and righteousness;
> I dare not trust the sweetest frame,
> But wholly lean on Jesus' name.
>
> On Christ, the solid rock, I stand;
> All other ground is sinking sand.

We have guarded against one error in interpreting Christ's parable: to think that we can have Christ's teachings without Christ. But we need to guard against the opposite error also: to think that we can have Christ without Christ's teachings. That is what Jesus is particularly warning against in Luke's version of the parable, for it is a reaction to those who, as He says, "call me, 'Lord, Lord,' and do not do what I say" (Luke 6:46). According to Jesus, we cannot have His ethics without Himself, but neither can we have Him without His ethics. We must build on both.

The context is very important at this point, for in both the Sermon on the Mount and in Luke 6 the parable comes as the conclusion to a substantial body of Jesus' ethical teaching. The most obvious case is the Sermon on the Mount. There it is found toward the end of chapter seven, after three chapters of moral instruction. The section in Luke is shorter, but it is parallel to Matthew 5-7. It begins with a brief version of the Beatitudes and includes such teachings as the need to love one's enemies and forego judging and condemning others. Of course, we are not to restrict the practice of Christ's teaching to what is found in those four chapters only. But if we want an example of what Jesus particularly had in mind as He spoke the parable, we can hardly do better than those items.

> Blessed are you who are poor,
>   for yours is the kingdom of God.
> Blessed are you who hunger now,
>   for you will be satisfied.
> Blessed are you who weep now,
>   for you will laugh.
> Blessed are you when men hate you,
>   when they exclude you and insult you
>   and reject your name as evil,
>   because of the Son of Man.
>
> Luke 6:20-22

"Rejoice in that day and leap for joy, because great is your reward in heaven. For that is how their fathers treated the prophets" (v. 23). The phrases "because of the Son of Man" and "that is how their fathers treated the prophets" make it clear that Jesus is not extolling poverty, hunger, sorrow, or rejection for their own sakes, as if there could be some virtue in those things. Rather, He is extolling them when they are endured for *His* sake or, as He says in the Sermon on the Mount, for the sake of "righteousness." Here is the blessedness of one who practices the teaching of Christ even to the point of personal deprivation or the hatred of others.

Such a person obviously has an ordering of life in which Christ, rather than himself, is the center. And with that change it is not hard to go and do the other things the Lord speaks about:

> "Love your enemies, do good to those who hate you, bless those who curse you, pray for those who mistreat you. If someone strikes you on one cheek, turn to him the other also. If someone takes your cloak, do not stop him from taking your tunic. Give to everyone who asks you, and if anyone takes what belongs to you, do not demand it back. Do to others as you would have them do to you. . . . Do not judge, and you will not be judged. Do not condemn, and you will not be condemned. Forgive, and you will be forgiven. Give, and it will be given to you. A good measure, pressed down, shaken together and running over, will be poured into your lap. For with the measure you use, it will be measured to you." [Luke 6:27-31, 37-38]

There is enough in those verses to keep any disciple of Christ busy for a very long time. It is precisely the practice of such things that is Christ's chief concern in this parable.

THE HOUSE WILL STAND

The life that Jesus holds before us is not appealing at first sight, for it is utterly opposed to the kind of self-seeking life the people of the world (and most of us) practice. And let us face it, it does have disadvantages. There *is* sorrow, deprivation, persecution. There is a great advantage to offset those drawbacks, however; namely, that a life built on Jesus and His teachings will stand—it will stand in the trials and testings of this life, and it will stand in eternity.

We are going to have tribulations. Those are our common lot, but the Christian who is building on Christ and whose mind is captive to the will of God can triumph over them gloriously (Rom. 5:3). The Book of Job contains a passage in which one of Job's comforters says, "Hardship does not spring from the soil, nor does trouble sprout from the ground. Yet man is born to trouble as surely as sparks fly upward" (Job 5:6-7). The image is highly poetic. It tells us that each generation can be compared to a stack of cordwood that is placed on the burning embers of the past. That is our destiny: to pass through fire and in time to be released by burning. Every child of Adam — you and I and countless millions of others — will experience sorrow, pain, suffering, disappointment, and eventually death.

What is the solution? Not escape, certainly; escape is impossible. The solution is to build on the sure foundation. Jesus says that although rains will fall, floods will rise, and winds will blow, the life that is constructed on Him will survive the blast and last forever.

That was true for Job. That was true for Moses and David and Isaiah and Jeremiah and all the other great Old Testament figures. It was true for Peter and James and John and Paul. Let me give you a more contemporary illustration.

Dr. Joseph Parker of London, the noted English preacher, who for many years proclaimed the Word of God in the great City Temple, tells in his autobiography that there was a time when he gave too much attention to the modern theories of his day. Men were reasoning and speculating and undervaluing the Word of God, and he found himself, as he read their books and mingled in their meetings, losing his grip intellectually upon the great fundamental doctrine of salvation alone through the atoning blood of the Lord Jesus Christ. But he tells us that there came into his life the most awful sorrow that he ever had to bear. His devoted wife, whom he loved so tenderly, was stricken, and in a few short hours was snatched away from him. He was unable to share his grief with others, and walking through those empty rooms of his home with a breaking heart, his misery felt for some footing in modern theory and there was none. "And then," he said, addressing a company of his Congregational brethren, "my brethren, in those hours of darkness, in those hours of my soul's anguish, when filled with doubt and trembling in fear, I bethought myself of the old gospel of redemption alone through the blood of Christ, the gospel that I had preached in those earlier days, and I put my foot down on that, and, my brethren, I found firm standing. I stand there today, and I shall die resting upon that blessed glorious truth of salvation alone through the precious blood of Christ."[2]

At that point Dr. Harry A. Ironside, from whom I have taken this illustration, adds: "On Christ, the solid Rock, I stand; all other ground is sinking sand."

There is one final point. We have spoken of building on a firm foundation, as a wise builder, and of building on sand, as a foolish builder. But at least those who do one or the other are building. The one may not be practicing, but he is hearing Christ's words. What of those who do not even hear, because they will not? If anyone is more foolish than the one who hears but will not practice, it is the one who refuses to hear at all.

Charles Spurgeon wrote of such people:

There are tens of thousands to whom the preaching of the gospel is as music in the ears of a corpse. They shut their ears and will not hear, though the testimony be concerning God's own Son, and life eternal, and the way to escape from everlasting wrath. To their own best interests, to their eternal benefit, men are dead; nothing will secure their attention to their God. To what, then, are these men like? They may fitly be compared to the man who built no house whatever, and remained homeless by day and shelterless by night. When worldly trouble comes like a storm those persons who will not hear the words of Jesus have no consolation to cheer them; when sickness comes they have no joy of heart to sustain them under its pains; and when death, that most terrible of storms, beats upon them they feel its full fury, but they cannot find a hiding place. They neglect the housing of their souls, and when the hurricane of almighty wrath shall break forth in the world to come they will have no place of refuge. In vain will they call upon the rocks to fall upon them, and the mountains to cover them. They shall be in that day without a shelter from the righteous wrath of the Most High.[3]

If you are in that class, do not be so foolish as to go on unprepared and so perish. Come to Jesus now. Believe on Him, and begin to build not merely for this life but for eternity.

2. H. A. Ironside, *In the Heavenlies: Practical Expository Addresses on the Epistle to the Ephesians* (Neptune, N.J.: Loizeaux, 1937), pp. 56-57.
3. Spurgeon, "On Laying Foundations," pp. 49-50.

Parables
of the
Christian Life

14

A TALE OF
TWO SONS

(Matthew 21:28-32)

"What do you think? There was a man who had two sons. He went to the first and said, 'Son, go and work today in the vineyard.'

" 'I will not,' he answered, but later he changed his mind and went.

"Then the father went to the other son and said the same thing. He answered, 'I will, sir,' but he did not go.

"Which of the two did what his father wanted?"

"The first," they answered.

Jesus said to them, "I tell you the truth, the tax collectors and the prostitutes are entering the kingdom of God ahead of you. For John came to show you the way of righteousness, and you did not believe him, but the tax collectors and the prostitutes did. And even after you saw this, you did not repent and believe him."

There is a connection between the last of the parables of wisdom and folly, in which some of Christ's hearers were saying "Lord, Lord . . ." while refusing to do what He said, and this first parable of the Christian life, in which a son promises to do what his father asks but does not do it. However, in the first case the people who professed without practicing were real people and the story was about men who build homes with or without foundations. In this case the teacher is part of the story, and the occasion that draws the story forth is the refusal of the religious leaders of Christ's day to respond to John the Baptist's teaching.

The story comes toward the end of Matthew, after the triumphal entry of Jesus into Jerusalem on what we call Palm Sunday. He had been received by the people with shouts of "Hosanna!" and "Blessed is he who comes in the name of the Lord!" That did not please the religious leaders, and it pleased them even less when Jesus came into the Temple area and drove out the merchants who were buying and selling. He said, "It is written . . . 'My house will be called a house of prayer,' but you are making it a 'den of robbers' " (Matt. 21:13).

The rulers began to question Him: "By what authority are you doing these things?" (v. 23).

Jesus replied by asking them about John the Baptist's authority. "I will also ask you one question. If you answer me, I will tell you by what authority I am doing these things. John's baptism—where did it come from? Was it from heaven, or from men?" (vv. 24-25). That question placed the rulers between the horns of a dilemma. If they denied that John's authority was from heaven, they would be discredited in the eyes of the people, for the people held that John was a prophet; that is, he spoke the words of God. On the other hand, if they acknowledged John's authority, they would be faulted by Jesus for their failure to believe in Him, since John testified that Jesus was the Messiah.

At last they took the coward's way out and said, "We don't know" (v. 27).

Jesus then replied, "Neither will I tell you by what authority I am doing these things" (v. 27). Then He told the story about the two sons. Each was told by his father to go and work in the vineyard. One said he would not, but afterward repented and went. The other said he would but did not. Jesus asked, "Which of the two did what his father wanted?" (v. 31).

They answered "The first."

Jesus then added this conclusion: "I tell you the truth, the tax collectors and the prostitutes are entering the kingdom of God ahead of you. For John came to you to show you the way of righteousness, and you did not believe him, but the tax collectors and the prostitutes did. And even after you saw this, you did not repent and believe him" (vv. 31-32).

TWO CHARACTERS

The context indicates how the parable of the two sons is to be taken. The son who professed to obey his father but did not actually do it represents the chief priests and elders; they had a reputation for being God's servants but rejected God's prophets. The son who first rejected his father's command but later did what he wanted represents the despised tax collectors and prostitutes, who had been in rebellion against God's standards but who in many instances repented of their particular sins and came to Jesus. Moreover, since the command of the father was to work in the vineyard, this is a parable, not merely of salvation—that is, of believing on Jesus—but also of Christian life and service. It asks, "Who are those who truly serve?" as well as "Who are God's children?"

Briefly put,

> The father is God; the vineyard is the church. The sons are two classes of men to whom the command to labor in the church comes from God: the first is the type of openly abandoned and regardless sinners, who on receiving the command of God defiantly refuse obedience, but afterward, on sober second thought, repent and become earnest in working the work of God; the second is the representative of the hypocrites who in smooth and polite phrase make promises which they never intend to keep, and who, never changing their mind, take no further thought either of God or of his service.[1]

Here, as in the last parable, Christ's emphasis is on *doing* or *failing to do* the will of the father, rather than on other issues. Take the case of the second son, who said, "I will, sir" but did not go into the vineyard. A person might reason from that that Jesus is suggesting it is improper to make promises to God, since we may not keep them. He might conclude, "I will make no promises to God, no profession of discipleship." That would be wrong. Jesus is not against profession. On the contrary, the Bible links confession to true belief in Jesus: "If you confess with your mouth, 'Jesus is Lord,' and believe in your heart that God raised him from the dead, you will be saved. For it is with your heart that you believe and are justified, and it is with your mouth that you confess and are saved" (Rom. 10:9-10). What Jesus is against is an insincere profession, that of one who cries, "Lord,

1. William M. Taylor, *The Parables of Our Saviour Expounded and Illustrated* (New York: A. C. Armstrong and Son, 1900), pp. 122-23.

Lord. . . ," but who does not do what He says.

Are you in that category? You cannot answer by saying that you have joined a church, affirmed the creeds, have a reputation as a good Christian, or even that you are a Christian worker or minister. You can do all those things and still be disobedient to God, just as the religious leaders were. They were active in all sorts of religious things. But they did not believe John the Baptist, they did not believe Jesus, and they were not working in God's vineyard. They were working in a vineyard of their own, building their own little kingdoms. You can only answer that question properly if you have believed on Jesus as your Savior and are now engaged in the specific work to which He has called you.

There is also the case of the other son, the first. He said no to the father, but afterward repented of his disobedient spirit and went to work in the vineyard. Here again, however, we must not think that Jesus was approving everything about him. To be specific, Jesus did not approve his initial disobedience. Sometimes we come across people who justify a disobedient or arrogant tongue by arguing (obviously enough) that that is just the way they are. They are straightforward, plain people who call things as they see them and let the chips fall where they may. They suppose that their arrogance is somehow all right just because they are open about it. They suppose they are not sinners just because they are not hypocrites.

They are like an adulterer who supposes that his adultery is less heinous because he lets his wife know, or the thief who supposes that he is less of a thief because he boasts about his thievery. In approving the eventual obedience of this first son Jesus was not approving his initial disobedience. The only thing that was good about him is that, although he had arrogantly defied his father when the command was first given, he later repented and did his father's will.

I make a point of that because there are people today, often young people, who think that it is all right for them to go their own way as long as they go God's way at some later point. They want to have fun now and serve God later—when they are too old to be of much use or when their opportunities for sound preparation are gone. Granted, it is better for them to sin now and repent later than for them to sin now and not repent at all. But it does not follow that there is not a better way than either. The best way is to come to Jesus early and serve Him both early and late. It is best to give your entire life to His service.

Besides, if you delay now, you have no guarantee that you will be able to come to Jesus later. You may, but sin takes its toll, and one of the things sin does is entrap us so that we cannot get free even if we wish to, and usually we do not even want our freedom. If God is speaking to you and you are saying no, you should know that, although it may be hard for you to say yes now, it will be even harder to say it the next time around—even assuming that God speaks to you again. The only safe thing is to give prompt and sincere obedience to God's call.

WORK IN THE VINEYARD

Having established the general meaning of the parable, let us now see what specific teaching it has for the Christian's life and service. The verse to be considered is verse 28, in which the father says to the first son, "Son, go and work today in the vineyard."

There are four important parts to this command. First, there is *work to be done,* for the father is reported as saying, *"Go and work today in the vineyard."* I do not know why it should be necessary to emphasize that, for the work to be done is so evident. But it is necessary, perhaps because we are so blind to the needs of others. In our day, thanks to the work of the great relief agencies, there is some sensitivity to the physical needs of the world's disadvantaged populations. Nearly a billion persons, one-fourth of the population of the world, live on less than $75 per year. At least 460 million are starving.

But great as that need is, there is an even greater need in spiritual matters where more than those are experiencing a famine of the Word of God. Of the four billion people on this planet it is estimated that approximately one billion identify themselves as Christians, another billion do not but may have heard the name of Jesus, and *more than two billion have never even heard His name.* Moreover, even among the one billion who identify themselves as Christians there are many who undoubtedly do not have a saving relationship to Jesus and many who do but who need much teaching to become spiritually strong.

In view of that it is ludicrous that so many of the large denominations are cutting back on missionaries. They say that the day of the missionary is over. But it is not! Their evaluation is different from that of the Lord, who said, "The harvest is plentiful, but the workers are few. Ask the Lord of the harvest, therefore, to send out workers into his harvest field" (Luke 10:2).

The second part of the Lord's command, expressed through the instruction of the father to his son, is that the work to be done is *God's work*. The son is told to "go and work today *in the vineyard.*" That is an especially important word to our generation, for many today are working—it is an age of work, an age of sometimes feverish activity—but most of what is done is not for God. It is work in *our* vineyards, for *our* profit, the end being *our* ease and glory. I am convinced that in any normal gathering of contemporary Christians the majority have never done any consistent work for God and are unlikely to do so unless their present understanding of discipleship or their present life-style changes. They do not serve in church offices. They do not teach Bible classes. They do not witness. They do not bring friends or neighbors to church. If the truth be told, they do not even pray or read their Bibles much. Yet they suppose all is well with them and that God is somehow pleased with their nonperformance. They would say that they have no time for those things, being so busy elsewhere.

Is that right? What are such persons to say to the Lord when they are asked to give an account of their lives? Will they not find themselves in the position of the second son? They have said, "Yes, Lord, I will do whatever you want," but they are working for nobody's benefit but their own.

The third point is that *the need is now.* That is why the father said, "Go and work *today* in the vineyard." It is interesting that God, who is eternal and who presumably has endless ages to do whatever He wishes, should emphasize the importance of doing work now; while we, who are creatures of a day and who are not even certain we will be around tomorrow, should procrastinate. We might think that God would delay and we should get immediately to work, but that is not how it is. We delay, and it is God who not only works now but also encourages us to work now.

William Taylor, from whom I have borrowed the four points in this section of the exposition, writes,

> Let us be faithful with ourselves here, and see if we are not involved in this condemnation. Are there not many among us who would shrink from saying to the Lord, "I will not," while yet we are habitually postponing the performance of duty and are daily increasing our arrears of service to him? Which of us will dare to say that yesterday, for example, he left nothing

undone of all that God in his providence put before him to be performed on his behalf? Let us be on our guard, therefore, in this matter; for procrastination grows upon us the more we yield to it. Our work accumulates, and our time for doing it diminishes, all because we are not fully alive to the importance of today. "Tomorrow," says the proverb, "is the day on which idle men work and fools reform." Let us show our industry by beginning to work for God now and our wisdom by reforming at once, for still the command runs, "Go work today"; and evermore, as we waver in our obedience thereto, the Holy Ghost repeats the warning, "Today, if ye will hear his voice, harden not your hearts."[2]

When we have responded to the urgency of our call by working for God today and not postponing our service until tomorrow, then we will be able to urge repentance and belief upon those to whom we are witnesses. Life is uncertain, and the opportunities a person has to come to Christ are limited.

On Sunday night, October 8, 1871, D. L. Moody was preaching in Chicago to the largest congregation he had ever addressed up to that time. His text was: "What shall I do then with Jesus who is called Christ?" At the end of the sermon he said something like this: "I want you to take this text home with you and turn it over and over in your mind. Next week we will be talking about Christ's death on the cross, and we will decide what to do with Jesus of Nazareth." Ira Sankey began to sing: "Today the Savior calls; for refuge fly. The storm of justice falls and death is nigh." But the hymn was never finished. While Sankey was singing there came a roar of fire engines on the street outside, and before morning Chicago lay in ashes. It was the night of the great Chicago fire.

Moody testified that to his dying day he regretted telling the congregation to wait until the next week to decide what to do with Jesus. He said,

> I have never dared to give an audience a week to think of their salvation since. If they were lost they might rise up in judgment against me. I have never seen that congregation since. I never will meet those people again until I meet them in another world. But I want to tell you of one lesson that I learned that night, which I have never forgotten, and that is,

2. Ibid., p. 131.

when I preach, to press Christ upon the people, then and there, and try to bring them to a decision on the spot. I would rather have that right hand cut off than give an audience now a week to decide what to do with Jesus.[3]

The fourth point of the father's instruction concerns *duty*, the duty of a son to do a father's bidding. He said, "*Son,* go and work today in the vineyard." If you are a Christian, there was a time when you were not a son. You had no family relationship to God. You were, at best, a disobedient subject of heaven's King. But God brought you into a family relationship. As Paul says, "You are no longer foreigners and aliens, but fellow citizens with God's people and members of God's household" (Eph. 2:19). You are now a son or daughter of God, and you have responsibilities along with the many family privileges. Should you not say constantly, as Jesus did, "I must be about my Father's business" (Luke 2:49, KJV)?

LET NONE DESPAIR

It is probably for the sake of that last point, the father-son relationship, that the parable ends with an emphasis on the coming of sinners to Jesus. The religious rulers were thought of as sons of God, but they did not value that relationship and consequently did not serve God. It was quite different with the tax collectors, prostitutes, and other sinners. They realized that a great gift was being conferred on them. So they did repent and serve enthusiastically.

There is encouragement for everyone in the conclusion. The devil will tell you that you have sinned too deeply to be received by God and that you might as well go on sinning. But Jesus stands over against the devil and brands that utterance a lie. He says, "Tax collectors and prostitutes *are* entering the kingdom." Moreover, they are entering ahead of the visibly religious people. He is not saying that the hypocrites cannot enter. They can. Anyone can come. But He is saying that in some ways it is easier for open sinners to believe on Jesus than it is for "religious" people, and for that reason He holds out hope for all. You need not despair, whoever you are. Simply turn from your sin—God will not save us *in* our sin; He saves us *from* it—and turn to Jesus. He is the Lamb of God who takes away the sin *of the world.*

3. From Clarence Edward Macartney, *Preaching Without Notes* (New York and Nashville: Abingdon-Cokesbury, 1946), pp. 24-25.

15

TWO STORIES ABOUT LAMPS

(Luke 8:16-18; 11:33-36)

"No one lights a lamp and hides it in a jar or puts it under a bed. Instead, he puts it on a stand, so that those who come in can see the light. For there is nothing hidden that will not be disclosed, and nothing concealed that will not be known or brought out into the open. Therefore consider carefully how you listen. Whoever has will be given more; whoever does not have, even what he thinks he has will be taken from him.

"No one lights a lamp and puts it in a place where it will be hidden, or under a bowl. Instead he puts it on its stand, so that those who come in may see the light. Your eye is the lamp of your body. When your eyes are good, your whole body also is full of light. But when they are bad, your body also is full of darkness. See to it, then, that the light within you is not darkness. Therefore, if your whole body is full of light, and no part of it dark, it will be completely lighted, as when the light of a lamp shines on you."

Years ago in America when many people traveled by train, and buggies were still common, there was a tragedy at a rural railroad crossing. A carriage containing an entire family was struck by an oncoming train and its occupants were killed. There was an inquest, and the man assigned to watch that particular crossing and warn travelers of the approaching trains was examined. They asked him if he was at the crossing that night, as he was supposed to be; he replied that he was.

"Did you know the train was coming?"

"Yes. It was right on time as always."

"Did you take your lantern and go out to meet it, as you were supposed to do?" the examiner continued.

"Yes."

"And did you wave it back and forth to warn that the train was coming?"

"Yes."

That was the heart of the examination, so after a few more routine inquiries the inquest was dropped. The conclusion was that it had been just one of those unfortunate accidents for which there was no known cause. Years went by, but at the time of his death the incident emerged again in the gateman's thinking. He was heard moaning over and over, "Oh, those poor people. Oh, those poor people." A friend asked what he was talking about, and when he explained that it was the accident at the railroad crossing many years before, his friend tried to reassure him. "But there was a careful investigation of that," his friend explained. "You were completely exonerated."

The gateman said, "But there was one question they didn't ask me. They didn't ask me if my lantern was lit." It had not been, and the death of the family in the carriage was the consequence.

LIGHT AND DARKNESS

Our Lord talked about lamps on quite a few occasions, generally using them to stress the responsibility of His disciples to others in this world. His basic teaching is in the Sermon on the Mount, where He called His disciples "the light of the world." He said, "People [do not] light a lamp and put it under a bowl. Instead they put it on its stand, and it gives light to everyone in the house. In the same way, let your light shine before men, that they may see your good deeds and praise your Father in heaven" (Matt. 5:15-16). This idea is elaborated on in other situations to make related but slightly different points. In particular, it is developed in two stories from Luke's gospel: one in a context of His teaching of His disciples (as in the Sermon on the Mount), one in a context of rebuking His enemies. The two stories begin almost identically, and both follow an identical outline. One says, "No one lights a lamp and hides it in a jar or puts it under a bed. Instead, he puts it on a stand, so that those who come in and see the light" (Luke 8:16). The other begins, "No one lights a lamp and puts it in a place where it will be hidden, or under a bowl. Instead he puts in on its stand, so that those who come in may see the light" (Luke 11:33). Each then applies the idea to a particular situation and concludes with a challenge. But interestingly enough, the situations are different and the challenge is different. In the first case, the image is applied to the life of Christ's disciples, stressing that they must give careful heed to His teachings so that they will represent the gospel well. In the second, the application is to unbelievers, and the challenge is to clear up their spiritual vision so that they can perceive the gospel.

Let us look at the first. After introducing the image, Jesus says, "For there is nothing hidden that will not be disclosed, and nothing concealed that will not be known or brought out into the open. Therefore consider carefully how you listen. Whoever has will be given more; whoever does not have, even what he thinks he has will be taken from him" (Luke 8:17-18).

Usually, when the Bible talks about something hidden that will be disclosed, or concealed that will be brought into the open, it is thinking of the secret sins of men and women and is saying that those will all be made known in the day of God's final judgment. That would be appropriate in a story dealing with light, for we can understand how the light of God might shine into the darkened recesses of our sinful hearts and expose what is there. That is not what Jesus is speaking of in this parable, however. Immediately prior to this He has been speaking of sowing the seeds of the gospel and of His own people's perceiving the meaning of His teachings. His conclusion is for those, His own, to listen carefully to what He says. In that context, the things that will be brought to light are not sins, but rather gospel teaching. It was to be known fully through Christ's ministry. His disciples were to listen carefully so that they might be able to hold out the light of salvation before the world.

There are several parts to this teaching. First, the world is in spiritual darkness. Second, Jesus is this world's light. Third, those who know Jesus are to become lights also. (He is the light-giver; we are to become light-bearers.) Fourth, we are to be lights by living and proclaiming the gospel.

The first part of Christ's teaching is that the world is in darkness, and the tragedy is that people prefer the darkness to God's light. Several years ago an old woman in the bush country of Africa said to a missionary, "You missionaries have brought us the light, but we don't seem to want it. You have brought us the light, but we still walk in darkness." She was speaking only of the life she knew, but her words aptly describe the reaction of everyone to the light of Christ and the gospel. Jesus was the light of the world when He was in the world. Today Christians are bearers of His light. But people still prefer darkness. They prefer their own sinful way of living to the perfect and holy standards of Christ.

Part of the problem is that most people will not even admit that. *Time* magazine once made some accurate remarks about the presence of evil in America:

> It is the particular heresy of Americans [it could have said "of everyone"] that they see themselves as potential saints more than as real-life sinners. . . . Today's young radicals, in particular, are almost painfully sensitive to these and other wrongs of their society, and denounce them violently. But at the same time they are typically American in that they fail to place evil in its historic and human perspective. To them, evil is not an irreducible component of man, an inescapable fact of life, but something committed by the older generation, attributable to a particular class or the "Establishment," and eradicable through love and revolution.[1]

Unfortunately, evil is an irreducible component of man, and it is no less real because most people are unwilling to acknowledge it.

The second part of Christ's teaching is that He is the light. That is not obvious in this particular parable, though Jesus explicitly claimed to be the light elsewhere (John 8:12; 9:5); rather, it is implied. Who is lighting the lamps of Christian witness if it is not Jesus, the source of all light? Who is disclosing the light of the gospel if not Jesus, who is the center and substance of that message?

One way we know that Jesus is the light is that He exposed the

1. *Time,* 5 December 1969, p. 27.

darkness that was around Him as no one had done previously. And, of course, people hated Him for it. Actually, the coming of Jesus into the world exposed the world's darkness, even where people thought they had the most light.

When I was very young I spent a number of summers at a Christian camp in Canada. Each summer my friends and I took several camping trips. The trips were fun, as I remember, but the sleeping accommodations were not. The ground was hard. Often it was damp. Generally there were rocks underneath the bedding. I remember lying awake, sometimes for most of the night, talking or fooling around with the other campers. During a particularly long night we would play with our flashlights. We would shine them in one another's eyes, and the game was to see which was the brightest. Usually the one with the brightest reflector or the largest number of batteries won. Obviously the game could only be played in the dark. When the sun came up the differences among the flashlights faded into insignificance by comparison.

That is what happened when the Lord Jesus Christ came into the world, and that is what men and women still experience when they meet Him. As long as we live in the darkness and are never exposed to God's light, we are able to compare the relative merits of human goodness and be totally oblivious to how much in darkness we are. We are able to see the differences among a three-battery character, a two-battery character, and one that has almost gone out. We rate others accordingly. But those distinctions fade away in the presence of the white light of the righteousness of Christ. He reveals the depth of our darkness.

YOU ARE THE LIGHT

The third point of Christ's teaching, indeed, the central one in this parable, is that His disciples are to be light also. How? We are creatures of the darkness ourselves—how can we be light? The answer is, by being lighted by Jesus or, to change the metaphor slightly, by reflecting His light. That is why Jesus speaks about a lamp; a lamp must be lit. It is why He called John the Baptist "a lamp that burned and gave light" (John 5:35). John's light came from Christ and reflected Him.

One of the greatest illustrations I have heard of that point was by

Donald Grey Barnhouse. He said that when Christ was in the world He was like the sun, which is here by day. But when the sun goes down the moon comes up. The moon is a picture of the church, of Christians. It shines, but it does not shine by its own light. It shines only because it reflects the light of the sun. Jesus said of Himself, "I am the light of the world" (John 8:12). But when He was thinking of the fact that one day He would be taken out of the world He said, "You are the light of the world" (Matt. 5:14). That is why the world is in such darkness today. At times the church is a full moon in the glow of revival, when men like Luther, Calvin, or Wesley are here. At other times the church is a new moon, and you can barely see it. But whether it is a full moon, a new moon, or only a waxing or a waning quarter it glows because of the sun. We can show light only if we reflect the real light of the Lord Jesus.

How can we do that? Here is where the Lord's fourth point comes in. It is only by learning from Jesus. We are to grow by His teaching, just as a plant grows by water and sunlight. Moreover, as He says, the one who grows thus will grow more, but whoever does not grow by listening and learning will become even weaker than he was previously. "Whoever has will be given more; whoever does not have, even what he thinks he has will be taken from him" (v. 18).

Do you listen to Jesus carefully? Do you grow by His teaching? If you do, you will function a bit like Jesus Himself when He was on earth. One thing that will happen is that your presence will begin to expose the darkness of this world, and you will be hated for it, as Jesus was. You will illuminate dishonest practices in business, gossip in the secretarial pool, loose talk and still looser morals at parties, corruption in local politics, racial prejudice, greed, selfishness, and other things. Those sins will appear darker even to non-Christians because of what you reveal of the holy character of Jesus.

You will also help faith grow, particularly among those of weak faith. Friends should grow because of what you know of Jesus. If you are married and have children, they should grow to full spiritual stature in your home.

Finally, you should see others turn to Jesus through your testimony. In his day the apostle Paul taught this by means of an illustration drawn from the Old Testament. In 2 Corinthians 3 and 4 Paul had spoken of Moses, and as he did so his mind turned to the imagery of light. When Moses was with God on the mountain his face shone with transferred glory as a result. The glory was so bright that later when Moses had come down from the mountain he had to cover his face so that it would not dazzle the people. Using that theme Paul argues that we, too, should shine with that glory as a result of spending time with Jesus. Others should be able to see Him as He is reflected by us. He concludes, "For God, who said, 'Let light shine out of darkness,' made his light shine in our hearts to give us the light of the knowledge of the glory of God in the face of Christ" (2 Cor. 4:6).

SEEING THE LIGHT

The second story about lamps is quite different, as we have indicated. But the point of the story follows naturally from the point of the first. Luke 11:33-36 is for unbelievers. There, after making an introductory statement about a lamp's being placed on a stand so that all may see it, Jesus continues, "Your eye is the lamp of your body. When your eyes are good, your whole body also is full of light. But when they are bad, your body also is full of darkness. See to it, then, that the light within you is not darkness. Therefore, if your whole body is full of light, and no part of it dark, it will be completely lighted, as when the light of a lamp shines on you" (Luke 11:34-36).

Again the context is helpful. Jesus had been talking to the crowds, among whom were some of His enemies. He had cast a demon out of a man, and they claimed that He had done it by the power of the devil—that is, that Jesus was an agent of Satan. Later they asked for a sign, and He replied that no sign would be given to that wicked generation except the sign of His coming resurrection. Those people had been seeing His miracles and would see the even greater miracle of the resurrection. But they were not believing— they were actually opposing him —and the reason for their disbelief was not a lack of evidence but rather their own warped vision that prohibited their seeing Christ clearly. His challenge was for them to change their outlook so that they would not stumble on in spiritual darkness forever.

That is what Jesus meant when He applied the image of a lamp to their eyes. It is as though He was talking of trimming the wick or polishing the glass. The light is shining; *He* is the light. But they needed to polish up their perception of Him. As one commentator says, "When the eye is sound and right and light is shining, the eye enables you to make full use of the light—you can see where you are, how to walk and how to do your work. But when there is something wrong with your eye you cannot make use of the light even when you are irradiated by the brightest light. Your whole body is then, as it were, wrapped in darkness."[2]

Here were people enveloped in spiritual darkness so that they could not perceive the light of the Lord Jesus Christ. They were so blind to Him that they imagined His works were done by Satan's power. Jesus told them to take heed to their eyes, to see that the light within is not darkness. Does that mean that they could regenerate themselves, that they could give themselves the spiritual vision they did not have? No. But it does not mean that they were to sit back and do nothing. Here we think of Christ's teaching in John 3. "This is the verdict: Light has come into the world, but men loved darkness instead of light because their deeds were evil. Everyone who does evil hates the light, and will not come into the light for fear that his deeds will be exposed" (John 3:19-20). Those men were doing evil. They did not see the light because they did not *want* to see it and thus be exposed as the sinners they were. To such people Jesus says, "Turn from your sin. Repudiate your evil way of life. Seek righteousness. And the light of the gospel will flood your soul and bring you to faith."

You cannot have sin and Jesus, too. Sin will keep you from Him. But if you want the light and will turn to it, you will find that He 's already shining and that God is already at work to save you through the gospel of our Lord and Savior Jesus Christ.

---

2. Norval Geldenhuys, *Commentary on the Gospel of Luke* (Grand Rapids: Eerdmans, 1977), pp. 337-38.

16

THE GOOD SAMARITAN

(Luke 10:25-37)

On one occasion an expert in the law stood up to test Jesus. "Teacher," he asked, "what must I do to inherit eternal life?"

"What is written in the Law?" he replied. "How do you read it?"

He answered: " 'Love the Lord your God with all your heart and with all your soul and with all your strength and with all your mind'; and, 'Love your neighbor as yourself.' "

"You have answered correctly," Jesus replied. "Do this and you will live."

But he wanted to justify himself, so he asked Jesus, "And who is my neighbor?"

In reply Jesus said: "A man was going down from Jerusalem to Jericho, when he fell into the hands of robbers. They stripped him of his clothes, beat him and went away, leaving him half dead. A priest happened to be going down the same road, and when he saw the man, he passed by on the other side. So too, a Levite, when he came to the place and saw him, passed by on the other side. But a Samaritan, as he traveled, came where the man was; and when he saw him, he took pity on him. He went to him and bandaged his wounds, pouring on oil and wine. Then he put the man on his own donkey, took him to an inn and took care of him. The next day he took out two silver coins and gave them to the innkeeper. 'Look after him,' he said, 'and when I return, I will reimburse you for any extra expense you may have.'

"Which of these three do you think was a neighbor to the man who fell into the hands of robbers?"

The expert in the law replied, "The one who had mercy on him."

Jesus told him, "Go and do likewise."

When I come to a story like the parable of the Good Samaritan, I like to paraphrase Christ's saying "the first shall be last and the last first" by noting that "the easy shall be hard and the hard easy." I mean that in some ways the parable of the Good Samaritan is the most straightforward of all the Lord's stories. It is clarity itself—the story of a Samaritan who showed mercy to the victim of a beating and robbery, and who thus acted as a "neighbor" toward him. We are to "do likewise." Yet the story is one of the hardest of the Lord's parables to expound.

TWO STORIES

To begin with, the story is actually *two* stories. That is, there is the story of the lawyer who asked the question that occasioned the parable, and there is the parable itself. Moreover, although the stories are related in that the second is an answer to a question raised in the first, they actually deal with different matters. The first concerns salvation. The second concerns God-pleasing conduct.

The parable begins with a question asked of Jesus by a certain lawyer: "What must I do to inherit eternal life?" (v. 25). The motive of the man was probably wrong, since we are told that he asked his question to "test" Jesus and later tried to avoid the personal application of Jesus' answer. But whatever his motive, the question is an important one. In fact, it is the most important question any person can ask. Bishop J. C. Ryle of England once wrote of that question,

It ... deserves the principal attention of every man, woman and child on earth. We are all sinners—dying sinners, and sinners going to be judged after death. "How shall our sins be pardoned? Wherewith shall we come before God? How shall we escape the damnation of hell? Whither shall we flee from the wrath to come? What must we do to be saved?"—These are inquiries which people of every rank ought to put to themselves, and never to rest till they find an answer.[1]

Unfortunately, those are questions very few people ask. Why is that? It is because in order to ask about salvation we must admit our need of salvation. We must admit we are sinners, in need of pardon for sin and deliverance from God's wrath. But we do not want to do that. We will confess to almost anything but depravity.

I think of some perceptive words on the subject by the Catholic Archbishop Fulton J. Sheen to the National Prayer Breakfast in January, 1979. Jimmy Carter was President at the time and was present for the breakfast. Bishop Sheen began by intoning, "Mr. President, Mrs. Carter, and Fellow Sinners . . ." It was a real attention grabber, and once he had their attention he went on to speak (as one might suppose on the basis of that opening) about sin. His point was that we do not want to admit our sinfulness but that we must. Indeed, that was the essential reason for a prayer breakfast, in his opinion. He said,

> We Americans are not very much given to the thought of sin. We may make a "mistake" as one public official admitted, or else we excuse our so-called anti-social behaviour because we were fed Grade B milk as children, or because of insufficient playgrounds, or because we were loved too much by a mother or too little by a father. Karl Menninger, the distinguished psychiatrist, has written a book entitled *Whatever Became of Sin?* The clergy dropped "sin" lest they offend their congregation; jurists then picked it up and turned "sin" into "crime," and finally, psychiatrists converted it into a "complex." The result is that no one is a sinner.[2]

That was true in Christ's time, too, of course. It is evident in the story. After the lawyer had asked Jesus his question, Jesus replied by directing his attention to the law. That is important in itself, for it shows Jesus' high regard for the Bible. He did not say, "Well, what

1. J. C. Ryle, *Expository Thoughts on the Gospels: St. Luke,* 2 vols. (Cambridge: James Clarke & Co., 1976), 1:370.
2. Archbishop Fulton J. Sheen, National Prayer Breakfast Address, delivered 18 January 1979.

do you think?" or "What do the rabbis say?" He referred to the Scriptures, asking, "What is written in the Law? . . . How do you read it?" (v. 26).

The lawyer answered correctly, as Jesus Himself had done on another occasion: "Love the Lord your God with all your heart and with all your soul and with all your strength and with all your mind" and "Love your neighbor as yourself" (v. 27). The first of these quotations is from Deuteronomy 6:5. The second is from Leviticus 19:18. Together they summarized the whole duty of man, first to God and then to his neighbor.

Jesus replied, "You have answered correctly. Do this and you will live." At that point it was evident to the lawyer, as it should be to anyone who thinks about it, that he had not done so. No one loves God "with all his heart and with all his soul and with all his strength and with all his mind." No one loves his neighbor "as himself." The lawyer should have said, "But I haven't done that. I can't. No one can. So what do I do now?" If he had allowed the conversation to go in that direction, Jesus could have responded with a presentation of the gospel. But the lawyer did not. He was convicted by Christ's words, but rather than admit his spiritual need he tried to "justify himself" by passing over the weightier of the two commands (to love God perfectly) and raising a quibble about the second. He asked, "And who is my neighbor?" It was in answer to that that the story of the Good Samaritan was given.

FOUR CLASSES OF PEOPLE

There are four classes of people in this second story—the victim, the victimizers, the indifferent, and the concerned—classes that cover nearly all of humanity. The important contrast is between the last two, for it answers the question, "And who is my neighbor?"

The Lord said that a certain man, presumably a Jew, was going down to Jericho from Jerusalem when he fell among thieves. They did what thieves still do today. They took his possessions and beat him, leaving him half dead. A priest was going by, the very type of man whom we might have supposed would be compassionate. But he did nothing. For whatever reason—too busy, scorn of the unfortunate, or fear of the same thing happening to himself—he simply glanced at the man and passed by.

Next came a Levite, also an educated person and of the upper class. But he, too, passed by. It seemed as though no one would help when, surprisingly, a Samaritan came and "took pity on him." This man might have had an excuse to pass by, because Samaritans were hated by Jews as being racially impure as well as members of a false religious sect. But that did not matter to the Samaritan in view of the victim's obvious need. He went to him, bandaged his wounds, and then took him to an inn where he took care of him and paid the innkeeper to continue his care after he himself had gone on.

Jesus asked, "Which of these three do you think was a neighbor to the man who fell into the hands of robbers?" (v. 36).

The lawyer replied, "The one who had mercy on him."

Jesus then said, "Go and do likewise."

When the lawyer asked his question—"And who is my neighbor?"—he was anticipating an academic discussion. He was like the woman at the well, whose sinful way of life had been exposed by Jesus and who tried to divert His line of questioning by a debate about religion: "Sir, I can see that you are a prophet. Our fathers worshiped on this mountain, but you Jews claim that the place where we must worship is in Jerusalem" (John 4:19-20). The lawyer did not love God perfectly. He did not love his neighbor perfectly. But he thought he could turn the pressure off by debating who actually qualified as his neighbor. Whatever Jesus said, he could (he thought), at least express another opinion, one easier to follow. Like most Jews of his time, he would define "neighbor" as a member of his own people and race.

But Jesus turned the problem around. Strictly speaking, He did not answer the lawyer's question. The lawyer was asking it in a form that made "neighbor" an object. Jesus made it a subject. He answered not "Who is my neighbor?" but rather "Who is the one who acts neighborly?" He was asking the lawyer, "Do you act as a neighbor to the person who needs your help?"

Let us put it in other terms and ask it of ourselves. We say, "Whom should I love?" or "How many people can I love?", thus hoping to limit our obligation. Jesus asks, "Do you love? Never mind whom; for if you do love, then your love will inevitably operate as it should when you come across the needy."

LOVE AND SACRIFICE

When the apostle Paul was writing about love in the great thirteenth chapter of 1 Corinthians, one of the things he said about it is that love is "not self-seeking" (v. 5). That characteristic is particularly well illustrated in Christ's story.

There are a number of things that might have hindered the Samaritan's acts of love, but they did not. It is in those areas that we particularly see love's "not-self-seeking" character. First, the Samaritan's neighborliness was not hindered by *a legalistic application of the law*, the precise thing that hindered the lawyer who asked the original question and possibly also hindered the priest and Levite of Christ's parable. Although the parable is not specific about it, I suspect that William Taylor is right when he suggests that the priest and Levite might have acted differently if the Bible contained a law that said, "If thou shalt see a man lying half dead upon the highwayside, thou shalt not pass him by unheeded."[3]

Those men prided themselves on keeping the law exactly; they were fanatics about it. But they were also mean-minded legalists who used their approach to Scripture to limit it and thus escape the law's true scope and meaning. If the law had said, "Help the poor man who is lying beside the road half dead," they would have done it—grudgingly perhaps. But because it only said, "Love your neighbor as yourself," they could debate who that elusive "neighbor" was and leave the poor man unattended.

Was that what the lawyer who asked the question was doing? No doubt. But it is what we do, too, particularly those of us who are good Bible scholars. We use our "expertise" to escape, to get off the hook. We exegete the meaning but excise the obligation. That should not hold us back. As Taylor says, "Instead . . . of waiting for any minute definition in the letter, like that which this lawyer expected when he said, 'Who is my neighbor?' let us show that, taught by the Holy Spirit and stimulated by the example of the Lord Jesus, we have learned to see that every sufferer whom we can assist has a claim of neighbor love upon us which we cannot repudiate without injuring him and dishonoring God."[4]

The second thing that might have hindered the Samaritan's show of love for the sufferer was *nationality or religion*. We do not know why the Lord had that in mind, but He must have wanted to stress

---

3. William M. Taylor, *The Parables of Our Saviour Expounded and Illustrated* (New York: A. C. Armstrong and Son, 1900), p. 230.
4. Ibid., p. 232.

in particular that the only one who stopped to help the disabled Jew was a Samaritan. About 750 years before the time of Christ the Assyrians had conquered the northern kingdom of Israel, where Samaria was located, had deported the Jewish population and then had resettled the area with their own people. It is not possible to transport an entire population, of course, so some Jews remained. (Perhaps they had hidden out in caves, bribed their captors, or escaped deportation in some other way.) Those Jews intermarried with the newcomers, thereby producing a race that was half-Assyrian and half-Jewish. To the Jews of the south that was an unforgivable sin. In their judgment the Samaritans had clearly forfeited their Jewish heritage.

Besides, they had their own religion. When the Jews of the south returned to Jerusalem after the Babylonian captivity and began to rebuild their Temple, the Samaritans offered to help. But because they were despised as half-breed outcasts, the Jews refused their offer, which angered the Samaritans enough to cause them to build their own Temple on Mount Gerizim. That became a rival Temple which in turn became the center for a rival religion.

The Jews hated the Samaritans for that and could not speak civilly of them. We notice, in fact, that when Jesus asked the lawyer which man had acted as a neighbor to the man who had fallen into the hands of the thieves, he could not even pronounce the word "Samaritan." He said instead, "The *one* who had mercy on him" (v. 36, italics added). But that was just the point. The outcast had acted as a neighbor though he had ample cause not to care, hated as he was, whereas the Jewish priest and Levite would not show mercy even to one of their own nationality. Christ's point is that love must transcend nationality, race, and religion.

We do have a first and special obligation to our own family: "If anyone does not provide for his relatives, and especially for his immediate family, he has denied the faith and is worse than an unbeliever" (1 Tim. 5:8). There is an additional, special obligation to Christians: "As we have opportunity, let us do good to all people, especially to those who belong to the family of believers" (Gal. 6:10). But that does not eliminate our obligation to care for needy ones in general. At the point of need we must be moved by the fact that the one involved is a creature made in the image of God, regardless of his or her profession, and not by whether the needy person qualifies as a member of our particular group.

Finally, the Samaritan was not deterred from his work by what must have been *great personal inconvenience*. That strikes home, because the inconvenience the Samaritan suffered was in both time and money, and we are most reluctant to give those up. We are told that the Samaritan interrupted his journey to take the injured man to an inn, where he cared for him overnight. The next day, he paid for his further care with two silver coins that he gave to the inn-keeper. Would we do that? Taylor writes perceptively that "some will give money to buy themselves off from personal exertion. Others will give their personal exertion to save their money. But in the instance before us, both were given; for, what genuine neighbor-love does, it will do thoroughly."[5]

We are not true followers of Christ until we are ready to give whatever is needed, and at personal cost. In short, it is only our feeding the hungry, our giving drink to the thirsty, our receiving the stranger, our clothing the naked, our caring for the sick, and our visiting the prisoners that shows us truly to be Christ's disciples (Matt. 25:34-36). Those things do not make us disciples, but their absence clearly shows that we are not.

That brings us back to the original question: "What must I do to inherit eternal life?" It brings us to the gospel.

The irrevocable word of God still remains valid, that he who observes the law perfectly will live. He who always loves God and his fellow-man will inherit eternal life. But alas, no man has ever been able to observe this law perfectly, nor can anyone do so. And because no imperfect observance of the law (however excellent it may be) can be accepted, and because the judgment of God that the soul that sins (even if only on a single occasion) shall die is just as irrevocable, we know that no man can ever inherit eternal life on the grounds of his own merit. But God be praised that Christ Jesus as man lived a life of complete love towards God and men and, as the entirely innocent one, endured death for us on the cross, forsaken by God, so that by faith we are absolved from the death we deserve and inherit eternal life. This, however, does not remove the obligaton to obey Jesus' words: "Go, and do thou likewise."

5. Ibid., p. 237.

But the difference is as follows: the Law has said, "Do this and thou shalt live," while Christ says: "I have given you eternal life through grace, and this new life in you will enable you to have real love towards God and your fellow-men and to carry it out in practice; so go forth and live a life of true love to God and to your fellow-men, through the power I give you."[6]

If we are Christians through faith in the finished work of Christ, we will live like that Samaritan.

6. Norval Geldenhuys, *Commentary on the Gospel of Luke* (Grand Rapids: Eerdmans, 1977), p. 312.

17

ON NOT GIVING UP

(Luke 11:5-13; 18:1-8)

Then he said to them, "Suppose one of you has a friend, and he goes to him at midnight and says, 'Friend, lend me three loaves of bread, because a friend of mine on a journey has come to me, and I have nothing to set before him.'

"Then the one inside answers, 'Don't bother me. The door is already locked, and my children are with me in bed. I can't get up and give you anything.' I tell you, though he will not get up and give him the bread because he is his friend, yet because of the man's persistence he will get up and give him as much as he needs.

"So I say to you: Ask and it will be given to you; seek and you will find; knock and the door will be opened to you. For everyone who asks receives; he who seeks finds; and to him who knocks, the door will be opened.

"Which of you fathers, if your son asks for a fish, will give him a snake instead? Or if he asks for an egg, will give him a scorpion? If you then, though you are evil, know how to give good gifts to your children, how much more will your Father in heaven give the Holy Spirit to those who ask him!"

Then Jesus told his disciples a parable to show them that they should always pray and not give up. He said: "In a certain town there was a judge who neither feared God nor cared about men. And there was a widow in that town who kept coming to him with the plea, 'Grant me justice against my adversary.'

"For some time he refused. But finally he said to himself, 'Even though I don't fear God or care about men, yet because this widow keeps bothering me, I will see that she gets justice, so that she won't eventually wear me out with her coming!' "

And the Lord said, "Listen to what the unjust judge says. And will not God bring about justice for his chosen ones, who cry out to him day and night? Will he keep putting them off? I tell you, he will see that they get justice, and quickly. However, when the Son of Man comes, will he find faith on the earth?"

George Mueller, the founder of the great Christian orphanage work in England in the nineteenth century, was a man of prayer. He knew the importance of keeping at a prayer even when the answer to it seemed delayed. When he was young he began to pray that two of his friends might be converted. He prayed for them every day for more than sixty years. One of the men was converted shortly before his death at what was probably the last service Mueller held. The other was converted within a year of his death. We, too, need to pray and not give up. We need to be like George Mueller.

Prayer is a difficult subject, of course—for many reasons. We do not know how our prayers relate to the sovereign, eternal counsels of God. We know that often we do not receive what we ask because we "ask with wrong motives" (James 4:3). But on other occasions we ask with right motives—at least we think so—and still we do not get what we ask. People have said that it is a lack of faith to pray for the same thing twice. God has heard it; He has promised to answer. To pray again is to show unbelief. But to be as "mature" in faith as that is to go beyond Christ who, on one occasion at least, prayed the same prayer repeatedly. In the Garden of Gethsemane He prayed over the space of several hours that "the cup" He was to drink might pass from Him (Matt. 26:36-46). It was of that event that the author of Hebrews later wrote, "During the days of Jesus' life on earth, he offered up prayers and petitions with loud cries and tears to the one who could save him from death, and he was heard because of his reverent submission" (Heb. 5:7).

TWO STORIES ABOUT PRAYER

That is what the two stories before us teach. The first is about a man who had a friend come to him late at night after a journey. He wanted to feed him something, but he had nothing to serve. So he went to a neighbor and asked, "Friend, lend me three loaves of bread, because a friend of mine on a journey has come to me, and I have nothing to set before him" (Luke 11:5-6). The friend did not want to be bothered. He had already gone to bed. But the petitioner kept pounding at the door, and eventually he got up and gave him bread, not because he was his friend but because of the seeker's persistence.

The Lord then said, in what has since come to be regarded as the great Magna Charta of believing prayer, "Ask and it will be given to you; seek and you will find; knock and the door will be opened to you. For everyone who asks receives; he who seeks finds; and to him who knocks, the door will be opened" (vv. 9-10).

Jesus also compared God to a human father, saying, "Which of you fathers, if your son asks for a fish, will give him a snake instead? Or if he asks for an egg, will give him a scorpion? If you then, though you are evil, know how to give good gifts to your children, how much more will your Father in heaven give the Holy Spirit to those who ask him!" (vv. 11-13).

The second story is the parable of the unjust judge. There was a judge who was unconcerned with giving justice. A widow in his town who had been unjustly treated, and who had no husband to plead her case, kept coming to him with the cry: "Grant me justice against my adversary" (Luke 18:3). He refused for a long time. But at last he gave her what she wanted, reasoning, "Even though I don't fear God or care about men, yet because this widow keeps bothering me, I will see that she gets justice, so that she won't eventually wear me out with her coming!" The Lord then drew this conclusion: "Will not God bring about justice for his chosen ones, who cry out to him day and night? Will he keep putting them off? I tell you, he will see that they get justice, and quickly. However, when the Son of Man comes, will he find faith on the earth?" (vv. 7-8).

SOME QUALIFICATIONS

If taken entirely by themselves, these stories are apt to be misunderstood. So before we speak further of perseverance in prayer, we need to place the subject in a wider biblical context. There are a number of points to consider.

First, the stories do *not* teach that God has gone to bed and is reluctant to get up and meet His children's needs. That may be true of Baal ("Maybe he is sleeping and must be awakened" [1 Kings 18:27]), but it is not true of the ever-watchful, all-knowing God of Israel. God is not an unjust judge. Merely to state it thus shows that the comparison is not one of likeness but of contrast. Indeed, that is the way Jesus spells it out in the application. We are evil, He says in the first parable. Even so, we will give to a person who persists in asking for something; and, if we are fathers, we will certainly give good gifts to our children. How much more will God give, since He is not at all evil or reluctant! The point of the second parable is that if even an unjust judge will give justice, because of a person's persistence, how much more will God who is not unjust but rather acts rightly!

Let us say it again; God is not unjust, and He is not asleep. He always does what is right; He is always awake to His children's needs. That is meant to be the greatest possible encouragement to us in our petitions.

Second, these stories do not teach that the privilege of prayer is for everyone. On the contrary, it is for God's children only. In the first story the person to whom the petitioner goes is his "friend" (v. 5), not a stranger. When the Lord applies the parable He speaks of God as "your Father in heaven," and God is not the Father of everyone. We see the same thing in the second story. In it there is no indication of any special relationship between the widow and the judge, but when Jesus applies the parable He makes clear what the limitation is by the term "his chosen ones." He says, "And will not God bring about justice for his chosen ones, who cry out to him day and night?" (v. 7).

These two parables as well as other teachings of the Lord about prayer cut to pieces the false doctrine of the universal fatherhood of God that has been so popular in this century. They teach that God is *not* the Father of all men. He is the Creator of all. But He is uniquely the Father of the Lord Jesus Christ and becomes the Father only of those persons who believe on Christ.

Jesus did not teach that only by implication. On one occasion He told some who thought they were God's children that they were actually children of the devil. Jesus had been teaching in Jerusalem and had made the statement, "You will know the truth, and the truth will set you free" (John 8:32).

The Jews answered him, "We are Abraham's descendants and have never been slaves of anyone. How can you say that we shall be set free?" (v. 33).

"I know you are Abraham's descendants," Jesus responded. "Yet you are ready to kill me. . . . If you were Abraham's children . . . you would do the things Abraham did" (vv. 37, 39). At that point the people grew angry and accused Jesus of being illegitimate. The Lord replied, "If God were your Father, you would love me, for I came from God and now am here. I have not come on my own; but he sent me. Why is my language not clear to you? Because you are unable to hear what I say. You belong to your father, the devil, and you want to carry out your father's desire" (vv. 42-44). Jesus put an end forever to the misleading and totally devilish doctrine that God is the Father of all men and all men are His children.

Let us submit to the Word of God. Let the truth of the Word sweep the mind clean of all such false ideas. There are two families and fatherhoods in this world. There is the family of Adam, into which all are born; and there is the family of God, into which some are reborn by faith in Jesus Christ. These were once children of darkness; now they are children of light (Eph. 5:8). They were dead in trespasses and sins; now they are alive in Christ (Eph. 2:1). They were once children of wrath and disobedience; now they are children of love and obedience (Eph. 2:2-3). These are God's children. Only they can come to God as their Father.

Third, these stories do not teach that we can pray for anything at all and know that God will give it, no matter how perseverant we are. Taken out of context they may seem to teach that, but in context they actually show something quite different. The first story follows immediately upon Luke's version of the Lord's Prayer. The disciples wanted to be taught how to pray, so Jesus instructed them, "When you pray, say:

" 'Father,
hallowed be your name,
your kingdom come.
Give us each day our daily bread.
Forgive us our sins,
    for we also forgive everyone who sins against us.
And lead us not into temptation.' "

Luke 11:3-4

Here is a prayer in which the petitioner first comes to God as his Father; second, desires that the name of God might be honored; third, seeks the coming of God's kingdom, and then fourth, prays for daily provision, forgiveness of sins, and deliverance from sin — and that not merely for himself, but for others also. Following that the parable of the friend who comes to another friend is given. In other words, the setting limits the kind of thing for which one might be supposed to pray. It will be nothing contrary to God's honor or kingdom. At the best, it will be for spiritual blessing and even that will be for others as well. In the parable, the plea for another, "Lend me three loaves of bread" (v. 5) clearly picks up on the earlier petition: "Give *us* each day our daily bread" (v. 3, italics added).

The second story is the same. Here the context concerns the delay of Christ's return at the end of the age (Luke 17:20-37). The plea of the widow for justice is parallel to believers' prayers for Christ's return. The teaching is that He will return, even though the event itself proves to be a long way off, and that in the meantime Christians are to continue to pray: "Amen. Come, Lord Jesus" (Rev. 22:20).

PRAYING IN GOD'S WILL

Having suggested some qualifications, we now turn back to the matter of perseverance in prayer and ask, For what, then, are we to pray? What can we pray for and know that God will eventually give it even though His granting of the request may be delayed? For what things should we persevere? Here our answer falls into two categories: first, things clearly said in Scripture to be the will of God for us; and second, things not explicitly stated as God's will for us individually or for any one particular point in history, but, nevertheless, things generally conformed to God's desires.

What things would be included in the first category? Many of the desires of God are disclosed for us in Scripture. In the Bible God's will is expressed in great principles. Take John 6:40 as an example. That verse can be called the will of God for all unbelievers. It says, "My Father's will is that everyone who looks to the Son and believes in him shall have eternal life, and I will raise him up at the last day." If you are not a Christian, God's will for you begins here. In one sense, God's will is wrapped up in the life and ministry of Jesus, and God will not take you on to other things until you believe in Him. He will not teach you spiritual calculus until you have mastered rudimentary math.

Another great passage that speaks explicitly of the will of God is Romans 12:1-2. It is an expression of God's will for a Christian. "Therefore, I urge you, brothers, in view of God's mercy, to offer your bodies as living sacrifices, holy and pleasing to God—which is your spiritual worship. Do not conform any longer to the pattern of this world, but be transformed by the renewing of your mind. Then you will be able to test and approve what God's will is—his good, pleasing and perfect will." Christians can accept as an unchangeable principle the truth that anything that contributes to growth in holiness and the surrender or renewal of the mind is an aspect of God's will, and anything that hinders growth in holiness is not.

A Christian may also claim God's promises, for they are certainly God's will for his life. James 1:5 says, "If any of you lacks wisdom, he should ask God, who gives generously to all without finding fault, and it will be given to him." If you ask for wisdom, you can be certain that you are praying in God's will and that your prayer will be answered.

Here is another: "Do not be anxious about anything, but in everything, by prayer and petition, with thanksgiving, present your requests to God. And the peace of God, which transcends all understanding, will guard your hearts and your minds in Christ Jesus" (Phil. 4:6-7). In other words, God wills that you have peace even in the midst of calamities, and He promises to give it to you if you lay your requests before Him.

Is someone saying, "But none of those verses covers the little things in life, things with which I am wrestling." Let me give you a verse for those. In Philippians 4:8 we read, "Finally, brothers, whatever is true, whatever is noble, whatever is right, whatever is pure, whatever is lovely, whatever is admirable—if anything is excellent or praiseworthy—think about such things." That means that you are to pursue the best things. If they are the best things for you, follow them. If not, go in another direction. Just be sure that you get your understanding of the will of God from Scripture.

PREVAILING PRAYER

Now we come to the second category. What about things that are in general conformity with God's desires, but for which we have no explicit promise that they will be true for us? What about George Mueller's friends, for example? It is God's general desire that people be saved ("He is patient with you, not wanting anyone to perish, but everyone to come to repentance," 2 Pet. 3:9), but there is no explicit promise in Scripture that those two friends of Mueller's, or anyone else's for that matter, are necessarily going to be saved. Was Mueller right to persist in prayer for them? Was he going beyond Scripture? Was he presuming to change the mind of the all-wise God, who perhaps would not have saved those two individuals had not Mueller prayed for them?

Here we must be most careful. On the one hand, we know that James says, "You do not have, because you do not ask God" (James 4:2). That seems to say that we ought to ask and keep on asking. On the other hand, we know that in the very next verse the writer goes on to say, "When you ask, you do not receive, because you ask with wrong motives" (v. 3). It is obviously possible to pray wrongly in situations, and if that is the case, should we ever persevere in praying?

I think the answer to that problem can be found along these lines. If you find yourself wanting to pray for something in this category—things in general conformity with God's will but not necessarily promised to you or anyone else—and find, as you pray, that your confidence in God's desire to answer your petition grows, then continue to pray; know that He will answer your prayers in due time. But if, as you pray, you do not find confidence and your ability to persevere in prayer weakens, then drop your petition. That does not necessarily mean that God will not do what you have asked for. Others may be praying. But it may mean that it is not His will to give you that petition or at least not to give it now.

That does not let you off the hook, however. You cannot say, "Well, I have no great burden to pray for anything, so I guess I don't need to persevere in prayer at all." That does not follow. Not every age is an age of great revival, but Jesus told us to "ask the Lord of the harvest . . . to send out workers into his harvest field" (Luke 10:2). If you can pray for nothing else, you can pray that God will raise up workers and send revival to our land.

The Great Awakening under Jonathan Edwards began with his famous call to prayer, and it was carried forward by prayer. The contemporaneous work of God among the North American Indians under David Brainerd, Edwards's friend, began in the nights Brainerd spent in prayer for God to effect that great work. In the seventeenth century a revival began in Ulster, Ireland that eventually spread throughout the whole country. How did it begin? It began with seven otherwise undistinguished ministers who committed themselves to pray regularly, fervently, and persistently for revival. The same was true of the Wesleyan revivals. At the time Wesley and Whitefield began their work, England was in a spiritual stupor, a moral abyss. Conditions were appalling. But a little group of believers began to pray, and God heard their prayer and sent a revival that transformed England and even spilled over into the new world. In the nineteenth century the revivals under D. L. Moody and others were carried on in a spirit of prayer. Can we not have that today? One writer says, "It is not necessary that the whole church get to praying to begin with. Great revivals always begin first in the hearts of a few men and women whom God arouses by his Spirit to believe in him as a living God, as a God who answers prayer, and upon whose heart he lays a burden from which no rest can be found except in importunate crying unto God."[1]

Have you nothing for which you can persevere in prayer? Then persevere in prayer for revival. Who can tell what God may do as a result of your prayer and the prayers of others whom He also calls to that service? The Bible says, "The prayer of a righteous man is powerful and effective" (James 5:16).

---

1. R. A. Torrey, *The Power of Prayer and the Prayer of Power* (Grand Rapids: Zondervan, 1955), pp. 245-46. The examples of revival I have mentioned are discussed at greater length by Torrey on pp. 240-46.

18

ON BEING THANKFUL

(Luke 7:36-50)

Now one of the Pharisees invited Jesus to have dinner with him, so he went to the Pharisee's house and reclined at the table. When a woman who had lived a sinful life in that town learned that Jesus was eating at the Pharisee's house, she brought an alabaster jar of perfume, and as she stood behind him at his feet weeping, she began to wet his feet with her tears. Then she wiped them with her hair, kissed them and poured perfume on them.

When the Pharisee who had invited him saw this, he said to himself, "If this man were a prophet, he would know who is touching him and what kind of woman she is—that she is a sinner."

Jesus answered him, "Simon, I have something to tell you."

"Tell me, teacher," he said.

"Two men owed money to a certain moneylender. One owed him five hundred denarii, and the other fifty. Neither of them had the money to pay him back, so he canceled the debts of both. Now which of them will love him more?"

Simon replied, "I suppose the one who had the bigger debt cancelled."

"You have judged correctly," Jesus said.

Then he turned toward the woman and said to Simon, "Do

you see this woman? I came into your house. You did not give me any water for my feet, but she wet my feet with her tears and wiped them with her hair. You did not give me a kiss, but this woman, from the time I entered, has not stopped kissing my feet. You did not put oil on my head, but she has poured perfume on my feet. Therefore, I tell you, her many sins have been forgiven—for she loved much. But he who has been forgiven little loves little."

Then Jesus said to her, "Your sins are forgiven."

The other guests began to say among themselves, "Who is this who even forgives sins?"

Jesus said to the woman, "Your faith has saved you; go in peace."

Not long ago a very special baby was baptized at Tenth Presbyterian Church. There was only one parent present, the mother. This woman was a Christian, but she had not been living close to the Lord and during the time of her spiritual drifting had conceived the child without being married. Her background had been secular, so her first thought was to get an abortion. After all, most of her friends seemed to be living that way. Why not? Even her doctor encouraged her to terminate the pregnancy. But her Christian friends objected. They argued that one sin is not improved by another—murder does not atone for fornication. It was a great struggle. At last she saw the issue in spiritual terms, canceled her appointment with the abortionist, had the baby . . . and was delighted. In her eyes the baptism was a public testimony to the grace of God in turning her life around and giving her the life and care of this now precious child.

Not everyone was in on the story, of course. Some who witnessed the baptism objected mildly: "Wasn't this a case of the church endorsing sin, or at least seeming to? Wasn't it an encouragement to others to be promiscuous?" The answer was that in other circumstances it may well have been, but that, in this case, the baptism really was a testimony to the grace of God in Christ to one of His children and of the woman's great and corresponding love for Him. She had been forgiven much, so she loved much. Her love was greater than that of many others who are not equally aware of the extent of their forgiveness.

A LIVING DRAMA

A situation similar to that became the basis of one of our Lord's great parables, involving a Pharisee, Jesus, and a sinful woman. We have a bad image of the Pharisees because of some of the things Jesus said about them—things richly deserved in most cases. But all were not that bad. We remember that Nicodemus was a Pharisee. He came to Jesus by night, and Jesus did not denounce him or his ways. Rather, Jesus tried to teach him about the necessity of the new birth. We have no evidence that Nicodemus ever was born again, but at the end of Jesus' life he was still there working with Joseph of Arimathea to obtain and then bury the body. The Pharisee in our story was something like that. He was not born again. He was not a believer in Christ. Still, he wanted to be sensitive to spiritual things and was at least respectful of Jesus as a perceptive and effective teacher. "Is He a true prophet?" the man was wondering. "Is He from God, or is He a charlatan?" The Pharisee—his name was Simon—decided to invite Jesus for dinner so he could get to know Him better.

Unfortunately, in reading the story we sense that the man was not quite as open as his invitation might lead us to suspect. It was customary for a host to see that a guest's feet were washed upon entering his home, for the guest's feet would have become dusty from the city streets. Simon had neglected to do that. Was it a simple oversight, perhaps justified because of his preoccupation with his guest? It is hard to think so. The story shows Simon to be skeptical. He was going to be a judge of Christ's character and calling. No doubt he deliberately postponed the courtesy until he could be sure Jesus was one he really wanted to honor.

The second character in the story is Jesus. He is on trial, as it were. It is an incongruous situation, for He is the true judge of men, not Simon. Yet Jesus goes to this man's house to be judged. Why? Because of grace. Jesus never held Himself aloof from anyone and honored even the most imperfect of motives. As one commentator writes, "It was part of his plan to accept hospitality whenever it was proffered to him, in order that he might thereby reach all classes and conditions of men. Therefore he did not decline the request of Simon, but went to his house, just, indeed, as he came to earth itself 'to seek and to save that which was lost.' "[1]

1. William M. Taylor, *The Parables of Our Saviour Expounded and Illustrated* (New York: A. C. Armstrong and Son, 1900), p. 212.

Last of all there is the woman. She has no name. We are only told that she had lived a sinful life in that town and that she had obviously repented of her sin. When "she learned that Jesus was eating at the Pharisee's house, she brought an alabaster jar of perfume, and as she stood behind him at his feet weeping, she began to wet his feet with her tears. Then she wiped them with her hair, kissed them and poured perfume on them" (Luke 7:37-38).

It is impossible to imagine that scene in terms of our western style of dining, but it is quite clear and natural for the way banquets were served in the east in Jesus' time. We know that the guests did not sit in chairs at a table, as we do. They reclined around a low table, leaning on their left arm and side and feeding themselves with their free right hand. We also know that banquets were public affairs to which many uninvited guests would come. They would not partake of the meal, but would be in the room and would stand or sit along the walls. In our culture that would be entirely out of line. But in the east it was an expected and even courteous thing to do. It was a way of honoring the host, acknowledging that he did indeed have an illustrious guest. And it would also be a way to listen in on the conversation. In some ways, the greater the bustle, the greater a success the evening would be.

Apparently this woman entered with the other uninvited guests. She would have been noticed, snubbed, scorned. All knew who she was. They did not want her company. But she was not there because they cared for her or she for them. She was there because of Jesus. She loved Him and knew that He loved and would forgive her. His love had melted her heart. So, as she stood there, she wept for her sin. She tried to show her love for Him by wiping His feet and anointing them with the perfume she had brought. When Jesus neglected to spurn the woman Himself, the Pharisee noticed it and thought he had his answer. If Jesus was a prophet, He would know what kind of woman she was—a sinner—and He would spurn her as the others had done.

A PARABLE PROPOSED

The Lord then told Simon a parable on being thankful. He said, "Simon, I have something to tell you. . . . Two men owed money to a certain moneylender. One owed him five hundred denarii, and the other fifty. Neither of them had the money to pay him back, so he canceled the debts of both. Now which of them will love him more?" (vv. 40-42).

The Pharisee answered, "I suppose the one who had the bigger debt canceled." Jesus told Simon that he had judged correctly, and then He applied the story (vv. 44-50). The climax came in verse 50, when Jesus told the woman, "Your sins are forgiven. . . . Your faith has saved you; go in peace."

It is not hard to see the lessons of this story, for they are there on the surface. They have to do with a lack of understanding and with ingratitude. Simon misunderstood everything—he misunderstood the woman, he misunderstood Jesus. He even misunderstood himself.

Simon misunderstood the woman because he was looking only on the outward appearance and not on her heart, which was what Jesus was seeing. This woman had been turned from sin to salvation. She had been brought to repentance and was now in the act of worshiping Jesus. Simon saw only her past, and therefore was willing to dismiss her without any further investigation.

Simon failed to understand Jesus, too. He was saying, "If Jesus is a prophet, He will know the character of this woman and will have nothing to do with her; since He allows her to proceed, He must not have the prophet's insight and must therefore be a charlatan." That is a good example of reasoning corrupted by sin. The major premise was right: if Jesus was a prophet, He would know the woman's character. But the minor premise was wrong: if He knew it, He would spurn her. Jesus did know her character, but He also knew her repentance. Besides, He came to earth to die for sinners like her.

Finally, Simon misunderstood himself. In looking down on the woman, he missed seeing that he himself was a sinner and every bit as much in need of the grace of God. Failure to see oneself as a sinner is the root cause of ingratitude—in Simon and in ourselves as well. Ours is an age of great ingratitude. There has probably never been a period of history in which people are as unthankful as they are in our day. Employers are not thankful for employees. Employees are not thankful for their employers. Husbands are not thankful for their wives, nor wives for their husbands. Children are not thankful for parents. Parents are not thankful for children. We are not thankful for friends.

Why is that? It is because we are thinking of ourselves, as the Pharisee was thinking of himself. We think we are better than others. We look down on others. We have no sense of sin. What we possess is not a cause for gratitude, because we think it is owed us. What we receive from others is not a cause of our appreciation of them. They are only acting as they should, considering who we are. The truth is, even then they are not measuring up to our due. Therefore, rather than appreciate what they are doing, we actually are resentful that they do not do more. Is that not the case? I think too often it is.

Even Christians do not escape it. I had an experience not long ago that brought my own ingratitude home to me. I had been in Pittsburgh for a conference and was flying home to Philadelphia early on a Sunday morning to preach at Tenth Presbyterian Church. I was catching the earliest plane and was up at 6:30 A.M. to get some breakfast in an airport restaurant. Nobody else was around except the girl behind the cash register in the restaurant. She was in a foul mood. When I paid for my food I did so with a twenty-dollar bill, since it was all I had. She asked rudely if I did not have something smaller. I said that I was sorry, but I did not. She grabbed the bill from me, banged my change on the counter, and stomped off, protesting about people who come through at 6:30 in the morning with twenty-dollar bills.

I was offended. I was thinking that I was her customer, after all. If she had trouble with twenty-dollar bills, she should get more change. The fault was hers, not mine. I got myself into quite a state. But then I sat down with my food, began to thank God for it, and realized that among the many things I should be thankful for was that girl, who undoubtedly needed to get up earlier than I in order to be there in the restaurant to serve me. She was ungrateful, since my money helped pay her salary. But so was I! I had missed being thankful for her service.

Why are we ungrateful? Because of sin! We consider ourselves better than other people. We will only become thankful (as Jesus wants us to be) when we recognize that we are *not* better than others, that we are alike in rebellion against God, and that everything we have—life itself, food, homes, friends, everything—comes to us solely from the grace of God who, if He did in this moment what justice requires, would instead of giving us those gifts be sending each of us to hell.

SHALL SIN ABOUND?

The question remains: Does not a gospel like this, a gospel of God's reaching out to save sinners, encourage sin? Cannot forgiveness be *too* free? The answer is no. A gospel like this does *not* encourage sin. It does precisely the opposite. By the power of this gospel prostitutes have been reformed. Drunkards have become sober. The proud have been humbled. Dishonest people have become models of integrity. Weak men have become strong—all because of the transformation wrought in them by the gospel of the grace of our forgiving God.

Here is a remarkable illustration from the life of Harry A. Ironside. Early in his ministry Ironside was living in the San Francisco Bay area, working with some Christians called Brethren. One evening as he was walking through the city he came upon a group of Salvation Army workers holding a meeting on the corner of Market and Grant Avenues. When they recognized Ironside they asked if he would give his testimony. So he did, giving a word about how God had saved him through faith in the bodily death and literal resurrection of Jesus.

As he was speaking, Ironside noticed that on the edge of the crowd was a well-dressed man who had taken a card from his pocket and had written something on it. As Ironside finished his talk the man came forward, lifted his hat, and very politely handed Ironside the card. On one side was his name, which Ironside recognized immediately. The man was one of the early socialists who had made a name for himself lecturing against Christianity. As Ironside turned the card over he read, "Sir, I challenge you to debate with me the question 'Agnosticism versus Christianity' in the Academy of Science Hall next Sunday afternoon at four o'clock. I will pay all expenses."

Ironside reread the card aloud and then replied somewhat like this.

I am very much interested in this challenge. Frankly, I am already scheduled for another meeting next Lord's Day afternoon at three o'clock, but I think it will be possible for me to get through with that in time to reach the Academy of Science by four, or if necessary I could arrange to have another speaker substitute for me at the meeting already advertised. Therefore I will be glad to agree to this debate on the following conditions: namely, that in order to prove that this gentleman has something worth debating about, he will promise to bring with him to the Hall next Sunday two people, whose qualifications I will give in a moment, as proof that agnosticism is of real value in changing human lives and building true character.

First, he must promise to bring with him one man who was for years what we commonly call a "down-and-outer." I am not particular as to the exact nature of the sins that had wrecked his life and made him an outcast from society—whether a drunkard, or a criminal of some kind, or a victim of his sensual appetite—but a man who for years was under the power of evil habits from which he could not deliver himself, but who on some occasion entered one of this man's meetings and heard his glorification of agnosticism and his denunciations of the Bible and Christianity, and whose heart and mind as he listened to such an address were so deeply stirred that he went away from that meeting saying, "Henceforth, I too am an agnostic!" and as a result of imbibing that particular philosophy found that a new power had come into his life. The sins he once loved he now hates, and righteousness and goodness are now the ideals of his life. He is now an entirely new man, a credit to himself and an asset to society—all because he is an agnostic.

Secondly, I would like my opponent to promise to bring with him one woman—I think he may have more difficulty in finding the woman than the man—who was once a poor, wrecked, characterless outcast, the slave of evil passions and the victim of man's corrupt living, perhaps one who had lived for years in some evil resort, utterly lost, ruined and wretched because of her life of sin. . . . But this woman also entered a hall where this man was loudly proclaiming his agnosticism and ridiculing the message of the Holy Scriptures. As she listened, hope was born in her heart, and she said, "This is just what I need to deliver me from the slavery of sin!" She followed the teaching until she became an intelligent agnostic or infidel. As a result, her whole being revolted against the degradation of the life she had been living. She fled from the den of iniquity where she had been held captive so long; and today, rehabilitated, she has won her way back to an honored position in society and is living a clean, virtuous, happy life — all because she is an agnostic.

"Now," he said, addressing the gentleman who had presented him with his card and the challenge, "if you will promise to bring these two people with you as examples of what agnosticism can do, I will promise to meet you at the Hall of Science at four o'clock next Sunday, and I will bring with me at the very least one hundred men and women who for years lived in just such sinful degradation as I have tried to depict, but who have been gloriously saved through believing the gospel which you ridicule. I will have these men and women with me on the platform as witnesses to the miraculous saving power of Jesus Christ and as present-day proof of the truth of the Bible."

Dr. Ironside then turned to the Salvation Army captain, a woman, and said, "Captain, have you any who could go with me to such a meeting?"

She exclaimed with enthusiasm, "We can give you forty at least, just from this one corps, and we will give you a brass band to lead the procession!"

"Fine," Dr. Ironside answered. "Now, sir, I will have no difficulty picking up sixty others from the various missions, gospel halls, and evangelical churches of the city. So if you will promise to bring two such exhibits as I have described, I will come marching in at the head of such a procession, with the band playing 'Onward, Christian Soldiers,' and I will be ready for the debate."

Apparently the man who had made the challenge had some sense of humor, for he smiled wryly and waved his hand in a deprecating kind of way as if to say, "Nothing doing!" and then edged out of the crowd while the bystanders applauded Ironside and the others.[2]

That is what the gospel of the grace of God in Christ does. It does not promote promiscuity. It is the power of God for the transformation of lives. It is when people recognize that they have been lifted from the dung heap of sin and made sons and daughters of the Most High — it is when they realize that, that lives are transformed and they become thankful to God and are determined to live in a way that shows their gratitude.

2. H. A. Ironside, *Random Reminiscences from Fifty Years of Ministry* (Neptune, N.J.: Loizeaux, 1939), pp. 99-107.

PARABLES OF JUDGMENT

19

A WRETCHED MAN'S WRETCHED END

Ch. Seaward Bk.

(Matthew 18:21-35)

Then Peter came to Jesus and asked, "Lord, how many times shall I forgive my brother when he sins against me? Up to seven times?"

Jesus answered, "I tell you, not seven times, but seventy-seven times.

"Therefore, the kingdom of heaven is like a king who wanted to settle accounts with his servants. As he began the settlement, a man who owed him ten thousand talents was brought to him. Since he was not able to pay, the master ordered that he and his wife and his children and all that he had be sold to repay the debt.

"The servant fell on his knees before him, 'Be patient with me,' he begged, 'and I will pay back everything.' The servant's master took pity on him, canceled the debt and let him go.

"But when that servant went out, he found one of his fellow servants who owed him a hundred denarii. He grabbed him and began to choke him. 'Pay back what you owe me!' he demanded.

"His fellow servant fell to his knees and begged him, 'Be patient with me, and I will pay you back.'

"But he refused. Instead, he went off and had the man

thrown into prison until he could pay the debt. When the other servants saw what had happened, they were greatly distressed and went and told their master everything that had happened.

"Then the master called the servant in. 'You wicked servant,' he said, 'I canceled all that debt of yours because you begged me to. Shouldn't you have had mercy on your fellow servant just as I had on you?' In anger his master turned him over to the jailers until he should pay back all he owed.

"This is how my heavenly Father will treat each of you unless you forgive your brother from your heart."

It has always bothered me to preach the same sermon more than once—not in the same place or to the same people, of course, but even in different locations. I have had to do that because of expanding invitations to preach and limited amounts of time for preparation. But I still do not like it. The only real comfort I have is knowing that preachers before me have repeated their sermons, too.

That was true of Charles Haddon Spurgeon. Few people prepared more original sermons than Spurgeon. He could get more out of a text than any man before or since, to my knowledge, and he probably published more sermons than anyone. He published one sermon per week for every year of his ministry, beginning in 1855 and continuing until his death in 1892. But at his death there were still so many unpublished Spurgeon sermons that they continued to be printed at the same rate for twenty-five more years, until 1917. There are more than 3,000 published sermons, all different. I am told, however, that when Spurgeon left the capital and went to the provinces, as he did on many occasions, he repeated his sermons there. Another example of unavoidable repetition was the great eighteenth-century evangelist George Whitefield. No one has ever preached more than Whitefield. It is estimated that he preached more than 18,000 formal sermons during his lifetime, plus almost that many informal sermons, which he called "exhortations." Whitefield preached as much as forty hours a week, on the average, and sometimes sixty. So, obviously, he repeated himself quite often.

The real justification for repeating a message, however, is the example, not of Spurgeon or Whitefield, illustrious as their examples may be, but of Jesus Christ who, as we know from a careful reading of the gospels, did just that. The substance of the Sermon on the Mount was repeated on more than one occasion (cf. Matt. 5-7 and Luke 6:17-49). Some of His sayings occur repeatedly in varying contexts (cf. Matt. 18:4; 23:12; Luke 14:11; 18:14). Even the parables must have been repeated, as is evident from a comparison of the story Jesus told Simon, the Pharisee, when He was in his house (Luke 7:41-42), and the story He told Peter when Peter asked Jesus a question about forgiveness (Matt. 18:23-25). The first version was brief. The second was longer. But essentially, each was only a variation on the other.

PETER'S QUESTION

It is this second story that we are to consider now. The earlier one was a response to Simon's disapproval of the woman's wiping Jesus' feet with her hair and anointing them with perfume. It was to answer the question, "Who will love most, the one who has been forgiven much or the one who has been forgiven little?" This story is an answer to Peter's question: "Lord, how many times shall I forgive my brother when he sins against me? Up to seven times?" (Matt. 18:21).

Peter must have been feeling quite good about himself in those days. It was now toward the end of Christ's ministry. Peter had been with Jesus for nearly three years and had undoubtedly learned much. In fact, just two chapters before this, when the group was at Caesarea Philippi and Jesus had asked the disciples, "Who do you say I am?" Peter responded correctly, "You are the Christ, the Son of the living God" (Matt. 16:16). Jesus had praised Peter for that answer, saying that it had been revealed to him by God. So even though Peter had said something very foolish afterward and had been as soundly rebuked for that as he had been praised for his earlier statement, Peter remembered his moment of insight and probably thought that he was making noteworthy progress in the school of Christ. In fact, so far had he come (in his own opinion) that he thought he was able to carry on a theological dialogue with Jesus. He picked his topic: forgiveness. Then he asked his question.

Peter was probably not drawing the question entirely out of the air. It was something that had been debated by the rabbis, and Peter was probably building on what he had heard when he asked his question. It is recorded in the Tractate Joma that Rabbi Jose ben Judah (c. 180 A.D.) said, "If a brother sins against you once, forgive him; a second time, forgive him; a third time, forgive him; but a fourth time, do not forgive him." No doubt Peter had heard discussions like that. So when he asked Jesus whether he should forgive a person as many as seven times, he may have felt that he was attaining the utmost heights of charity. After all, the rabbis said that a person should be forgiven only as many as three times. Peter was more than doubling that. What did he expect Jesus to answer? Maybe he expected Him to say, "That is very kind of you, Peter, but I don't think it will be necessary to go quite that far. Maybe four or five times will be enough."

Man's thoughts are not God's thoughts, however, and Peter had certainly misread the situation. Jesus' answer was, "No, Peter, not seven times, but seventy-seven times" (or possibly seventy times seven, or 490 times). His point was that our forgiveness of others should be unlimited.

We tend to look down on Peter at this point, faulting him for so misreading the mind of Christ, and we suppose that we would do better. But we should not think that. For one thing, Peter was at least asking the question. He realized that it was the spirit of his master to forgive and that he had an obligation to forgive also, as Jesus did. He may not have understood the full measure of that spirit he was of, but he was at least trying. Do we try? Or to put it another way, do we forgive even as many as the seven times about which Peter was speaking, not to mention the seventy-seven or 490 times suggested by Christ? Can you think of anyone who, in the last week or month or year, you have consciously forgiven for the same offense as many as seven times? You may have, but you probably have not. So at least grant Peter this: he had only been in Jesus' school for three years and had a great deal yet to learn, but he had at least learned that much. Some of us are barely matriculating in that school and are therefore quite far from graduating even from the rudiments of Christ's teaching.

JESUS' ANSWER TO THE QUESTION

Jesus told Peter a story to illustrate His point. A certain king wanted to settle accounts with his servants, so he called in one who had an enormous debt: ten thousand talents. It is hard to estimate exactly what that was worth, and it may in fact only mean the largest debt conceivable, "ten thousand" being one of the largest common numbers and a "talent" being the largest denomination of currency. However, if we do estimate it in dollars, we derive some interesting results. A talent was seventy-five pounds, so ten thousand talents would be 750,000 pounds. We do not know whether they were talents of gold or silver. But since Jesus is trying to exaggerate the contrast between this great debt and the relatively small debt of verse 28, we may suppose that He was thinking of the greater of the two talents, namely, gold. In troy weight there are twelve ounces to a pound. So we are now dealing with 750,000 times 12, or 9 million ounces of gold. Assuming that gold is selling at about $400 an ounce, we come to a figure of $3,600 million (three trillion six hundred million dollars). That is beyond our comprehension, which is precisely Christ's point. It is an astronomical debt, entirely beyond this servant's or anybody else's capacity to pay.

Since the servant was unable to pay, the king was going to have him, his wife, and his children sold into slavery and his goods sold on the open market to pay as much of the debt as possible. But hearing that, the man fell on his knees and begged, "Be patient with me, and I will pay back everything" (v. 26). He could not, of course, but the king had pity on him and canceled the obligation.

This man then found a fellow servant who owed him money, only one hundred denarii. A denarii was a day's wage for a common laborer, so that was approximately a third of a year's wages. Assuming (in our terms) that a low wage might be twelve or fifteen thousand dollars per year, it was only four or five thousand dollars. That was a significant amount of money, but it was a pittance compared to the enormous debt the first servant had incurred. Yet when the man with the smaller debt begged for time to repay it, which he could presumably have done, the wretched first servant hardened his heart and had the other thrown into prison.

The other servants heard what had happened and told the king. The king called the first man in and demanded, "You wicked servant, I canceled all that debt of yours because you begged me to. Shouldn't you have had mercy on your fellow servant just as I had on you?" (vv. 32-33). Then, according to Jesus, his master turned him over to the jailers until he should pay back all he owed.

At that point the story is finished, and we might wish that Jesus had stopped right there. But He had this final disturbing word: "This is how my heavenly Father will treat each of you unless you forgive your brother from your heart" (v. 35). That is troubling. Indeed, it is so troubling that many have tried to see if they cannot get rid of its disturbing implications. For one thing, it seems to imply a "works" salvation. That is, if you forgive others (a work), you will be forgiven. That seems contrary to the doctrine of justification by faith. Or again, even if it does not teach that, the parable seems to imply a continuation in grace by means of works. We may be saved by grace; but if we fail to act in an upright manner, God may cancel His forgiveness and have us thrown into hell anyway, just as the king had his wicked servant jailed. Since that is all unacceptable, Bible students have devised a number of ways of getting off the hook.

As I have read the various commentaries I have found at least three different ways of trying to do that.

First, some commentators apparently believe that *Jesus did not mean what He said.* They regard the parable as simple hyperbole, as an exaggerated statement given for its emotional or rhetorical effect. According to those scholars, Jesus did not mean to say that God would send us to hell if we do not forgive our debtors, but only that forgiveness is an extremely important matter and that we ought really to be forgiving. We *should* forgive others just as God has already forgiven us. But if we do not, that does not mean we are not saved or that we will lose our salvation.

That approach is a bit childish, for it is just what children do. When a mother is about to go out and instructs her children what is to be done in her absence, she says, "I have to go to the store for a few minutes. I want you to use the time when I'm gone to straighten up your rooms. Make your beds. Hang up your clothes. Put the toys back in the toy box. Don't waste the time watching television. Do you understand that?"

"Yes," the children answer.

"And you're going to do it?"

"Yes."

"You're sure? You're not going to put it off?"

"Oh, no," the children say, "we'll do it." The mother goes out.

When she comes back the rooms are exactly the way they were and the children are watching television. What do they say when she asks why they haven't cleaned up their rooms? They say, "Rooms? Rooms? Did you want us to clean up our rooms? We must have misunderstood you. We thought you wanted us to do it tomorrow."

The second way of trying to escape Christ's words is by *applying them to someone else*. According to that view, Jesus obviously meant what He said, but His words do not apply to people living in this age. Jesus' teaching was true for Jews living under the law, but it is not true for us. We are justified by faith apart from works. God's forgiveness does not depend in any measure on our forgiveness of others and is, in fact, not even linked to it.

That is like speeding down a highway and then, when you see the police car coming with his siren sounding and the light flashing, hoping that he is going after someone else. It is not to someone else but to *us* that Jesus is speaking.

Each of the above approaches is found in evangelicalism, but the third approach is not. It is that of liberalism, which instead of trying to get off the hook, actually delights in it by *throwing out the rest of the New Testament*. The liberal says, "Here we are getting to the heart of that beautiful and simple gospel that Jesus actually taught. He is not teaching the later Pauline doctrine of justification by faith in a so-called work of atonement. This is merely that beautiful teaching of doing to others as we would want them to do to us. We want God to forgive us. So should we want to forgive others. Since God does forgive us, we should understand Christ to be saying that the essence of religion is in God's being nice to us and our being nice to others. He is the forgiving Father of all; and, since He is, we ought to treat all men as brothers."

But of course, Jesus is not repudiating Paul. In fact, as is evident even on a most casual reading, Jesus is saying that if we do not forgive others, God is going to send us to hell. That is not the gospel of liberalism! Obviously, another way of understanding His words is required.

What we have to recognize is that in this one story Jesus is not giving the whole of biblical theology. What He says is true enough, namely, that there is an unbreakable connection between God's forgiveness of us and our forgiveness of other people. That is intended to snap us out of any lethargy we may have and confront us with the life-changing power of the gospel. But it does not mean that we are saved by forgiving others or that salvation, once acquired, can be lost. Jesus is not excluding the other parts of the gospel message. He is merely saying that, whatever else is involved (and much more *is* involved), forgiveness at least must be part of the picture.

Although we are justified by faith apart from works of the law, being justified is not the only thing that happens to us in salvation. In fact, it is not even the first thing. Justification is by faith, so faith at least comes before it. And since, as Jesus said to Nicodemus, we cannot "see" or "enter" the kingdom of God unless we are born again (John 3:3, 5), regeneration or the new birth must come before entering or believing. That means that no one believes on Christ and is justified who has not already been given a new nature, namely, the nature of the Lord Jesus Christ Himself. That is God's own forgiving nature. So although that nature does not manifest itself all at once, if we are justified we will have that nature of God that will increasingly and inevitably express itself in forgiveness, just as God for Christ's sake has forgiven us. We will be able to pray, "Forgive us our debts, as we also have forgiven our debtors" (Matt. 6:12).

The Lutherans says: "We are justified by faith alone, but not by a faith which is alone." It is always faith *and* life: first, the life of God within; then faith; then, the expression of the inner, divine life in what we do. The conclusion is: if we do not forgive, we are not forgiven. We are not justified. We are not God's children, regardless of what our profession may be.

The parable of the forgiven but unforgiving debtor makes three points. First, there is a judgment coming. Jesus did not pass over that teaching. He spoke of forgiveness, but He also spoke clearly of what happened to the wretched man in His story. He was cast into prison until he should pay back all he owed. That judgment hangs over everyone who has not experienced God's forgiveness through Christ. Second, there is forgiveness. God *does* forgive. God sent Jesus to be the basis for that forgiveness. Third, the only sure proof of a person's having received God's forgiveness through true faith in Jesus is a transformed heart and a changed life.

How do we get that down into the practical areas of our lives, so that we actually begin to treat others as we have been treated? It is by standing before the thrice holy God and thus seeing ourselves as the vile sinners we are—vile and yet forgiven through the death of God's own beloved Son. That awareness should humble us so that we have simply no other option but to be forgiving to others from our heart.

20

THE WICKED TRUSTEES

(Matthew 21:33-46)

"Listen to another parable: There was a landowner who planted a vineyard. He put a wall around it, dug a winepress in it and built a watchtower. Then he rented the vineyard to some farmers and went away on a journey. When the harvest time approached, he sent his servants to the tenants to collect his fruit.

"The tenants seized his servants; they beat one, killed another, and stoned a third. Then he sent other servants to them, more than the first time, and the tenants treated them the same way. Last of all, he sent his son to them. 'They will respect my son,' he said.

"But when the tenants saw the son, they said to each other, 'This is the heir. Come, let's kill him and take his inheritance.' So they took him and threw him out of the vineyard and killed him.

"Therefore, when the owner of the vineyard comes, what will he do to those tenants?"

"He will bring those wretches to a wretched end," they replied, "and he will rent the vineyard to other tenants, who will give him his share of the crop at harvest time."

Jesus said to them, "Have you never read in the Scriptures:

" 'The stone the builders rejected
has become the capstone;
the Lord has done this,
and it is marvelous in our eyes'?

"Therefore I tell you that the kingdom of God will be taken away from you and given to a people who will produce its fruit. He who falls on this stone will be broken to pieces, but he on whom it falls will be crushed."

When the chief priests and the Pharisees heard Jesus' parables, they knew he was talking about them. They looked for a way to arrest him, but they were afraid of the crowd because the people held that he was a prophet.

The first of Christ's great parables of judgment, which we looked at in the last chapter, shakes us out of our lethargy. It was meant to demolish presumption. In that parable Jesus taught that unless there has been a noticeable change in our lives, so that we now forgive others as we have been forgiven, we dare not assume that we have been born again even if we can give the right verbal answers to biblical questions. We are not saved by a transformed life; but if we have been saved by the mercy of God in Christ received through faith alone, transformation will follow as surely as spring follows winter or day follows night.

That parable did not examine the depth of the human problem, however, though it suggested it. It did not show in explicit enough terms that our natural mistreatment of others actually betrays a hatred of those other persons and that this in turn is an expression of our hatred of God. That point is made in the parable to which we come now.

The parable of the wicked trustees tells how men who had been selected to manage a vineyard for its owner mistreated the owner's servants and eventually killed his son. The father is God; the son is Jesus; the servants are the prophets. So the story shows that sinful men are so virulent in their hatred of all others, including God, that they murder God's servants and Son and would naturally murder God Himself if He stooped to put Himself in their grasp. What are the two great commandments? The first is: "Love the Lord your God with all your heart and with all your soul and with all your mind." The second is like it: "Love your neighbor as yourself" (Matt. 22:37,

39; cf. Deut. 6:5; Lev. 19:18). But on the basis of this story it is correct to say that man in his sinful state does precisely the opposite. He hates the Lord his God with all his heart and with all his soul and with all his mind, and he hates his neighbor as he hates himself.

GOD'S VINE

When Jesus began His story by telling how a landowner planted a vineyard, put a wall around it, dug a winepress, and built a watchtower, He was pressing the parable home upon His Jewish audience. Israel was the "vine" of God, and everything Jesus said in that opening picture was known to have been applied to Israel in the Old Testament. Isaiah had written, "My loved one had a vineyard on a fertile hillside. He dug it up and cleared it of stones and planted it with the choicest vines. He built a watchtower in it and cut out a winepress as well" (Isa. 5:1, 2). Jeremiah had recorded, "I had planted you like a choice vine of sound and reliable stock" (Jer. 2:21). Ezekiel declared, "Your mother was like a vine in your vineyard planted by the water; it was fruitful and full of branches because of abundant water" (Ezek. 19:10). The psalmist had written beautifully, "You brought a vine out of Egypt; you drove out the nations and planted it. You cleared the ground for it, and it took root and filled the land. The mountains were covered with its shade, the mighty cedars with its branches" (Ps. 80:8-10).

That imagery was well known to Christ's hearers. So when He told the story of the landowner's vineyard there could be no doubt in their minds that He was speaking of them and of those who had responsibility for their spiritual development.

That fact tempts us to dismiss the parable as applying only to them and therefore not to ourselves. But let us say at the start that if that is the way we are interpreting Christ's remarks, we are misreading Him utterly. Jesus told the story in that way because He was speaking to Jews. But would He not have made it equally pointed if He was telling it to us? He may have used another image—we do not know what it might have been. Or He might simply have said that we, too, may be compared to vines, as Israel was. Has He not planted Americans in our land? Has He not fenced us in? Has He not watered and cared for us? Has He not built a watchtower? Has He not sent tenants to care for us and present our choice fruits to Him when He returns for them? Of course He has. Yet we have not been faithful, any more than Israel was faithful.

In speaking to His Jewish audience, Jesus focused on the way God's servants had been and would be treated. In that we have both history and prophecy. In the days of Elijah, Jezebel murdered the Lord's prophets in large numbers. In the reign of Joash the people stoned Zechariah, the son of Jehoiada. Isaiah, the greatest of all the prophets, was sawn assunder by order of Manasseh, according to Jewish tradition. The tombs of many of those men were in the valley of Kidron, within a short walk of where our Lord was speaking, so anyone could easily have verified that the treatment of the prophets was as the Lord said.

The author of Hebrews wrote, "Others [of the prophets] were tortured and refused to be released, so that they might gain a better resurrection. Some faced jeers and flogging, while still others were chained and put in prison. They were stoned; they were sawed in two; they were put to death by the sword. They went about in sheepskins and goatskins, destitute, persecuted and mistreated— the world was not worthy of them. They wandered in deserts and mountains, and in caves and holes in the ground" (Heb. 11:35-38). Who is it who did those things to the prophets? It was the Jews, the very people to whom Jesus was speaking.

Christ's parable was also prophecy. It not only recounted what had happened. It foretold what those very people, the descendants of those who had killed the prophets, would do to Him. We speak of Jesus as being meek and mild. We refer to Him as the embodiment of love. We refer to His many works of healing the sick, raising the dead, curing the lepers. And those are true descriptions. He was all those things. But was He loved for it? On the contrary, He was hated because, at the same time that He was doing those good things, He was also the representative of God and the people hated Him for His Godlike characteristics.

NATURALLY GOD'S ENEMIES

Years ago the greatest theologian this country has ever produced, Jonathan Edwards, wrote a discourse that developed this theme at length. It was entitled "Men Naturally Are God's Enemies" and was based on Romans 5:10 ("For if, when we were God's enemies, we were reconciled to him through the death of his Son . . ."). Most of us, when we take a text like that, focus on the good part—in this case, on the wonder of the death of Christ. Edwards did not go about things in that way. He saw that no one could appreciate the death of Christ, the second part of the verse, until he understood that he was an enemy of God, the first part. So in that discourse he examined how we are God's enemies until regenerated.

We are God's enemies in several ways, says Edwards. First, we are enemies *in our judgments*. We have mean opinions about Him. Edwards uses an illustration here, asking: What do you do when you are present in some gathering and a friend of yours is attacked? The answer is that we go to his or her defense. And how is it when an enemy is praised? In that case, we introduce whatever negative factors we can and put down anything in that person that might be thought praiseworthy. So it is in people's judgments of God, Edwards argues,

> They entertain very low and contemptible thoughts of God. Whatever honor and respect they may pretend, and make a show of toward God, if their practice be examined, it will show that they certainly look upon him as a Being that is but little to be regarded. The language of their hearts is, "Who is the Lord, that I should obey his voice?" (Exod. 5:2), "What is the Almighty, that we should serve him? And what profit should we have if we pray unto him?" (Job 21:15). They count him worthy neither to be loved nor feared. They dare not behave with that slight and disregard towards one of their fellow creatures, when a little raised above them in power and authority, as they dare, and do, towards God. They value one of their equals much more than God, and are ten times more afraid of offending such, than of displeasing God that made them. They cast such exceeding contempt on God, as to prefer every vile lust before him. And every worldly enjoyment is set higher in their esteem than God. A morsel of meat, or a few pence of worldly gain, is preferred before him. God is set last and lowest in the esteem of natural men.[1]

1. Jonathan Edwards, "Men Naturally Are God's Enemies," in *The Works of Jonathan Edwards*, 2 vols. (Edinburgh and Carlisle, Pa.: Banner of Truth, 1974), 2:131.

The second way in which we show that we are enemies of God is *in the natural relish* of our souls. Relish is an old-fashioned word, but it means "likes" or "desires." Here Edwards means that we do not naturally take to God. In fact, the opposite is the case. By nature we find Him and His attributes repugnant.

This is where Edwards discusses our hatred of the four great attributes of God—holiness, omniscience, power, and immutability—which I have often referred to in echoing Edwards. He says of unsaved people,

> They hear God is an infinitely holy, pure, and righteous Being, and they do not like him upon this account; they have no relish of such qualifications; they take no delight in contemplating them. . . . And on account of their distaste of these perfections they dislike all his other attributes. They have greater aversion to him because he is omniscient and knows all things, and because his omniscience is a holy omniscience. They are not pleased that he is omnipotent, and can do whatever he pleases, because it is a holy omnipotence. They are enemies even to his mercy, because it is a holy mercy. They do not like his immutability, because by this he never will be otherwise than he is, an infinitely holy God.[2]

That explains why men and women will not have much to do with God, why they try to keep at such great distance from Him. I have a neighbor who is so adverse to God that one cannot even begin to witness to her. The moment the name of God comes up, she crys out, "Don't talk to me about God!" She is even adverse to letting her six-year-old daughter hear His name mentioned. It is why people will not go with you to church, will not read Christian books, will not pray. If the truth be told, it is why even Christian people have such a difficult time with some of these items.

Third, Edwards says that people are enemies of God *in their wills*. That is, the will of God and their wills are set at cross purposes to each other. What God wills, they hate. What God hates, they desire. Edwards says that is why they are so opposed to God's government. They are not God's loyal subjects, as they should be, but are opposed to His rule in this world. Their whole desire is expressed by the psalmist: "Let us break [God's] chains . . . and throw off [his] fetters" (Ps. 2:3).

2. Ibid.

Fourth, *the affections of the natural man* flare out against God. Edwards was aware that in prosperous times, when God seems to leave men alone and their plans are not disturbed, they manage for the most part to keep their evil affections toward Him hidden. They will even be a bit condescending in such times, as if from the throne of their own universe they might throw God a tip. But let them be crossed, let something go wrong, and their malice burns against Him. "This is exercised in dreadful heart-risings, inward wranglings and quarrelings, and blasphemous thoughts, wherein the heart is like a viper, hissing and spitting poison at God. And however free from it the heart may seem to be, when let alone and secure, yet a very little thing will set it in a rage. Temptations will show what is in the heart. The alteration of a man's circumstances will often discover the heart."[3] Edwards argued that those true affections will be seen most clearly when people are cast into hell. There will be no new corruption then, only less restraint on what had been present all along. But their hatred of God will burn continually.

Fifth, men are God's enemies *in their practice.* Here Edwards gets close to the main point of Christ's parable. For he says that although men and women cannot injure God, because He is so much above them, they nevertheless do what they can. They oppose themselves to God's honor, persecute His prophets, seek to thwart His work in this world and, in general, "list under Satan's banner" as willing soldiers.

What is to be done with such persons? That is precisely the question Jesus Himself asked of those who were listening to His parable. He could have given the answer Himself. He could have said, "Because of their wicked behavior, the owner of the vineyard will return and destroy those tenants." But Jesus did not apply it that way. Instead, He turned to the very people He was accusing of being such tenants and said to them, "Tell me, what will the owner do when he returns? You render judgment. What is the proper response to such wicked and inexcusable behavior?"

The people rightly replied, "He will bring those wretches to a wretched end, and he will rent the vineyard to other tenants, who will give him his share of the crop at harvest time" (v. 41). In rendering that judgment they spoke their own doom.

Here I think of the title of another of Jonathan Edwards's ser-

---
3. Ibid.

mons: "The Justice of God in the Damnation of Sinners." When most people hear that title today they are quite taken back and ask themselves, "What kind of person must Jonathan Edwards have been to have talked like that? What kind of a person would link justice to damnation?" But Jonathan Edwards was not the originator of such thoughts. They come from the words of the Pharisees and scribes as they pronounced judgment on themselves in replying to Christ's question. Moreover, that is the judgment you and I must render on ourselves if we are honest. What would you say if Jesus asked His question of you: "What do you think the owner of the vineyard should do?" Unless we are absolute hypocrites or absolutely ignorant, we would answer as the leaders of Jesus' day did and thus, likewise, render judgment on ourselves. We are such people, and that is our doom.

Hear the Lord's own judgment. After listening to what the men of His time thought should be done, he concluded, "Did you never read in the Scriptures: 'The stone the builders rejected has become the capstone; the Lord has done this, and it is marvelous in our eyes'? Therefore I tell you that the kingdom of God will be taken away from you and given to a people who will produce its fruit. He who falls on this stone will be broken to pieces; but he on whom it falls, will be crushed" (vv. 42-44).

At the end of his own study of this parable William Taylor, a great Bible teacher in New York at the turn of the century, spoke of three great points to the parable. It contains: 1. our greatest privilege, 2. our greatest sin, and 3. our greatest doom.

The *greatest privilege* is to have the kingdom of God entrusted to us. That is what happens when the kingdom of God is preached. It is placed within our grasp for receiving, feeding upon, and entering into. If someone offered you the privilege of becoming the President of the United States, it would not compare with the privilege of receiving the kingdom of God. If someone offered you the privilege of becoming a multi-millionaire, it would not compare with the privilege of becoming a son or daughter of the Most High.

The *greatest sin* is to reject that kingdom, which is to reject Jesus Christ. Jesus is not here today for us to kill Him. But we do what we can unless we are made anew by God. We reject His claims, and above all we reject His lordship over our lives.

The *greatest doom* is to be crushed by the kingdom of that very

Christ who is offered to us in salvation. When Jesus refers to being crushed by "this stone" I think He is referring to the vision Nebuchadnezzar had in the days of the prophet Daniel. Nebuchadnezzar had a dream in which he saw a statue representing four successive world kingdoms. At the end of the vision a stone came and struck the statue, grinding it to pieces, and then the stone became a huge mountain that filled the whole earth (Dan. 2). The stone is Christ. The mountain is His kingdom. So Jesus is saying to the people of His day, "You can be part of that kingdom and thus grow up with Me and fill the earth. That will happen by decree of the Most High God, My Father. Or you can stand against that kingdom and be broken."

The judgment of God is not to be taken lightly, because God is not to be taken lightly. The God who offers salvation now is the God who will judge in righteousness hereafter. If you will not have Him now as Savior, in the day of His grace, you will have Him as your Judge when you stand before His throne at the final judgment. Now is the day of grace. Come to Him. Come now. Even as He spoke those words, the Lord Jesus Christ was on the way to the cross to die for such as will have Him. Come, and be among that believing band.

21

UNPROFITABLE SERVANTS AND UNPROFITABLE GOATS

(Matthew 25:14-46)

"Again, it will be like a man going on a journey, who called his servants and entrusted his property to them. To one he gave five talents of money, to another two talents, and to another one talent, each according to his ability. Then he went on his journey. The man who had received the five talents went at once and put his money to work and gained five more. So also, the one with the two talents gained two more. But the man who had received the one talent went off, dug a hole in the ground and hid his master's money.

"After a long time the master of those servants returned and settled accounts with them. The man who had received the five talents brought the other five. 'Master,' he said, 'you entrusted me with five talents. See, I have gained five more.'

"His master replied, 'Well done, good and faithful servant! You have been faithful with a few things; I will put you in charge of many things. Come and share your master's happiness!'

"The man with the two talents also came. 'Master,' he said, 'you entrusted me with two talents; see, I have gained two more.'

"His master replied, 'Well done, good and faithful servant! You have been faithful with a few things; I will put you in charge of many things. Come and share your master's happiness!'

"Then the man who had received the one talent came. 'Master,' he said, 'I knew that you are a hard man, harvesting where you have not sown and gathering where you have not scattered seed. So I was afraid and went out and hid your talent in the ground. See, here is what belongs to you.'

"His master replied, 'You wicked, lazy servant! So you knew that I harvest where I have not sown and gather where I have not scattered seed? Well then, you should have put my money on deposit with the bankers, so that when I returned I would have received it back with interest.

" 'Take the talent from him and give it to the one who has the ten talents. For everyone who has will be given more, and he will have an abundance. Whoever does not have, even what he has will be taken from him. And throw that worthless servant outside, into the darkness, where there will be weeping and gnashing of teeth.'

"When the Son of Man comes in his glory, and all the angels with him, he will sit on his throne in heavenly glory. All the nations will be gathered before him, and he will separate the people one from another as a shepherd separates the sheep from the goats. He will put the sheep on his right and the goats on his left.

"Then the King will say to those on his right, 'Come, you who are blessed by my Father; take your inheritance, the kingdom prepared for you since the creation of the world. For I was hungry and you gave me something to eat, I was thirsty and you gave me something to drink, I was a stranger and you invited me in, I needed clothes and you clothed me, I was sick and you looked after me, I was in prison and you came to visit me.'

"Then the righteous will answer him, 'Lord, when did we see you hungry and feed you, or thirsty and give you something to drink? When did we see you a stranger and invite you in, or needing clothes and clothe you? When did we see you sick or in prison and go to visit you?'

"The King will reply, 'I tell you the truth, whatever you did for one of the least of these brothers of mine, you did for me.'

"Then he will say to those on his left, 'Depart from me, you who are cursed, into the eternal fire prepared for the devil and his angels. For I was hungry and you gave me nothing to eat, I was thirsty and you gave me nothing to drink, I was a stranger and you did not invite me in, I needed clothes and you did not clothe me, I was sick and in prison and you did not look after me.'

"They also will answer, 'Lord, when did we see you hungry or thirsty or a stranger or needing clothes or sick or in prison, and did not help you?'

"He will reply, 'I tell you the truth, whatever you did not do for one of the least of these, you did not do for me.'

"Then they will go away to eternal punishment, but the righteous to eternal life."

It is impossible to think of Christ's parables of judgment without thinking at once of the three great parables occurring in Matthew 25: the parables of the five wise and five foolish virgins, the talents, and the sheep and the goats. Each of them makes similar points, so the cumulative effect of the three stories is particularly strong. They occur in the last great body of teaching by Jesus recorded in Matthew's gospel. At this point Jesus is about to go to the cross. His disciples will see Him no more. But He reminds them that the day is coming when He will return as Judge of all men and that all who are wise should prepare to meet Him in that judgment.

One of those parables has already been studied: the parable of the wise and foolish virgins. That is because of its unique emphasis on human wisdom and folly. We considered it along with other parables on the same theme: the rich fool (Luke 12:13-21), a shrewd man of the world (Luke 16:1-9), and the wise and foolish builders (Luke 6:46-49). The two remaining parables of judgment are to be studied now.

A COMING JUDGMENT

I propose to take the five most obvious points of these parables. First, there is to be a day of future reckoning for all people. That is so obvious both from the stories of Jesus and from our experience of life that it seems almost juvenile to stress it. But it must be stressed, if only because most people think in precisely opposite categories. Jesus spoke of judgment being obvious, but they think of judgment being the most irrational and least-to-be-anticipated thing in the world. What do most people think of when one speaks of dying? Most probably do not want to think of it at all, of course; they are not certain what, if anything, lies beyond death's door. If they do speak about it, assuming that something does lie beyond this life, most people today think of the afterlife in good terms. At the very least they think of something like a continuation of life as we know it. Or, if it will not be that, it must be something better. Very few consider that it may be something worse. They cannot imagine God to be a God of judgment.

That relatively new development has caused R. C. Sproul to speak of the current doctrine of "justification by death." It used to be that Protestants and Catholics argued over justification. Protestants said that it is by faith alone *(sola fide)*. Catholics said that justification is by faith plus works *(fide et operae)*. But today that disagreement is outmoded in the minds of most people. To get to heaven all one has to do is die. One is "justified" by death alone.

In that our contemporaries are irrational, as they are in most other spiritual matters. This is an evil world. All sins are not judged in this world, nor are all good deeds rewarded. The righteous do suffer. The guilty do go free. If this is a moral universe, that is, if it is created and ruled by a moral God, then there must be a reckoning hereafter in which those tables are balanced out. The good must prosper, and the evil must be punished.

In most theological volumes on eschatology (the last things) there are three great points of emphasis: the return of Christ, the resurrection of the body, and the final judgment. But of the three, the only one that is truly reasonable is the last. There is no reason why Jesus should return again. He came once and was rejected. If He should write us off and never again give so much as a thought to this planet, it would be totally understandable. It is the same with the resurrection: "Dust you are and to dust you will return" (Gen. 3:19). If that is all there is, who can complain? We have had our lives. Why should we expect anything more? There is nothing of logical necessity in either of those two matters in and of themselves. But judgment? That is the most logical thing in the universe, and both of these stories say quite clearly that there will be a final day of reckoning.

In the first case, it comes when the "master of those servants returned and settled accounts with them" (Matt. 25:19). In the second, it is when "the Son of Man comes in his glory, and all the angels with him" (v. 31).

JUDGMENT BY WORKS

The second point of the stories is the emphasis on works, indeed, on judgment by works. That is surprising, and it troubles Protestants especially. We have been taught that salvation is by grace through faith apart from works, and here the judgment is on the basis of what people have done or not done. In the first case, it is the use or disuse of the talents given to the servants by their master. In the second, it is the care or neglect of those who were hungry, thirsty, strangers, naked, sick, or imprisoned.

We must not forget at this point that there has been an earlier story, the parable of the five wise and five foolish maidens, in which the emphasis has been on the faithful watching and waiting of the wise young women for the bridegroom. Their watching and waiting corresponds to faith. So we cannot take these accompanying stories as teaching that faith in Christ is unnecessary. Christ believed in faith. Still, these stories do round out the picture by showing what kind of faith it is that actually waits for the bridegroom. It is not a dead faith. A dead faith saves no one. It is a living faith. In that Jesus is one with the apostle James, who said, "What good is it, my brothers, if a man claims to have faith but has no deeds? Can such faith save him? Suppose a brother or sister is without clothes and daily food. If one of you says to him, 'Go, I wish you well; keep warm and well fed,' but does nothing about his physical needs, what good is it? In the same way, faith by itself, if it is not accompanied by action, is dead" (James 2:14-17).

Usually James is contrasted with Paul at this point. But we remember that Paul also said, "To those who by persistence in doing good seek glory, honor and immortality, he [God] will give eternal life. But for those who are self-seeking and who reject the truth and follow evil, there will be wrath and anger. There will be trouble and distress for every human being who does evil: first for the Jew, then for the Gentile; but glory, honor and peace for everyone who does good: first for the Jew, then for the Gentile. For God does not show favoritism" (Rom. 2:7-11).

Does that mean we are saved by works after all? Does it mean that the theology of the Reformation is wrong? No, but it is a statement of the necessity of works following faith — if we truly are regenerate. It is the point made in our study of the parable of the unforgiving servant (Matt. 18:21-35). As we said there, an unbreakable connection exists between what we believe and what we do, because we believe the gospel only because we are regenerate, and regenerated people will inevitably begin to live out the superior moral life of Christ. No one believes on Christ who has not been given a new nature, the nature of Jesus. So although that new nature does not show itself all at once, if we are justified we will have it and it will increasingly and inevitably express itself in forgiveness of and service to others, just as God has forgiven and served us. We are not justified by works. But if we do not have works, we are not justified. We are not Christians.

There is a warning for us here, which we did not see in the story of the unforgiving servant. When Jesus spoke of the men who were given talents by their master and who used them either wisely or not at all, He showed that some of the master's servants were given more than others and that some were given less. One man was given five talents; he used them to gain five more. A second was given two talents; he used those to gain two more. The last servant was given one. He was judged, but not for failing to gain as much as those who had been given more. He was judged for failing to use what he had. He hid his talent in the ground and was condemned for it.

We need to remember that when we find ourselves making comparisons between Christians. It is true, as this story teaches, that the people of God will do good works. They will diligently use the talents God has entrusted to them. But they will not all do it in the same way, on the same level, or to the same observable degree. So although God will judge the performance or nonperformance of those deeds, it ill behooves us to do so. Who are we to say that someone else is insufficiently serving or even hiding his talent in the ground? He may not be doing what we are doing, but he may be doing something far greater, which only our own sin blinds us from observing. Here is where the words of Paul should be applied: "Who are you to judge someone else's servant? To his own master he stands or falls. And he will stand, for the Lord is able to make him stand" (Rom. 14:4).

ALL MOUTHS STOPPED

Now let's qualify our qualification, or warn against our warning. The warning applies in our consideration of other people, whom we are not fit to judge. *But it does not apply to ourselves.* On the contrary, we must be rigorous with ourselves. We must not think that a poor or nonexistent performance will be excused.

That brings us to the third obvious point of the stories: the failure of all excuses before God. As we read them we find that the people who were confronted by the Lord's return made manifold excuses, just as people make excuses for their wickedness today. The man who had been given one talent and had hidden it in the ground explained that he had not done more because he knew the nature of his master too well: "Master, I knew that you are a hard man, harvesting where you have not sown and gathering where you have not scattered seed. So I was afraid and went out and hid your talent in the ground. See, here is what belongs to you" (vv. 24-25). The man claimed knowledge of his master's character as an excuse for failing to do what the master desired. It was a foolish thing, but do not many today do the same? They use justification theology to excuse the obligation to care for others practically. They use knowledge of predestination to excuse their call to evangelize. They use perseverance as an excuse for being lazy.

What did God say to that servant? He said that if he was right about his master's character, he should have worked all the harder. And He called him wicked and lazy—wicked because of his unjustified slander, and lazy because that was the real reason for his zero-growth performance! By that standard, what wicked persons must there be in our churches! How lazy some of us must be!

The second story shows us another excuse. In that parable the wicked are judged because they have not cared for Christ's brothers. But they reply, "Lord, when did we see you hungry or thirsty or a stranger or needing clothes or sick or in prison, and did not help you?" (v. 44). They complain that they did not see Jesus in those who were needy. To Jesus that is no excuse at all. He says, "Whatever you did not do for one of the least of these, you did not do for me" (v. 45).

You can get away with giving excuses to other people—to your boss, your parents, your pastor. But do not think that you can get away with giving excuses to God. The apostle Paul wrote that in the day of God's judgment "every mouth [will] be silenced and the whole world held accountable to God" (Rom. 3:19). There will not be even a single protest when the Judge takes the bench.

SURPRISE! SURPRISE!

I have been to a few surprise parties in my life when the person for whom the party was being given was really surprised. Usually they have not been, because they have noticed the clandestine preparations or someone has unwittingly "let the cat out of the bag." But sometimes the surprise has really come off. I think when I read these judgment stories that there really will be a surprise for many in the day of judgment, and it will not be a pretend surprise either. Many, if not all, will be absolutely astounded at Christ's judgment.

That is true in each of these stories, even the one about the ten maidens. The five who are left outside knock on the door and call out, "Sir! Sir! Open the door for us!" and are utterly surprised when the door is not opened. The man who has failed to use his talents is equally surprised. He expected to be rewarded. So also with the goats, who have failed to serve others as they think they would have served Christ. They say, "When did we see you hungry or thirsty or a stranger or needing clothes or sick or in prison, and did not help you?" (v. 44). They mean that they would have done everything that is required if they had only seen Christ, but since they did not see Him they cannot imagine why they are being judged. Each of those individuals expects to be rewarded. Each expects to enter into the joy of the Lord.

Here, I suppose, is the perfect portrait of the visible but unbelieving church. It will be the end of many who in their lifetime called out "Lord, Lord," but did not do the things Jesus said. Are you one? We would not dare to say that if the Lord had not said it first, but on His authority we must say that many who worship in apparently Christian congregations, who consider themselves good Christians, supposing that all is well with their souls, will be surprised utterly in that day.

If such will be banned from God's presence, ought we not to do as Peter says and "make [our] calling and election sure" (2 Pet. 1:10)? Just before that Peter had spoken of how it must be done. He had spoken of efforts to add goodness to faith, knowledge to goodness, self-control to knowledge, perseverance to self-control, godliness to perseverance, brotherly kindness to godliness, and love to brotherly kindness. But then he concludes, "If you *do* these things, you will never fall, and you will receive a rich welcome into the eternal kingdom of our Lord and Savior Jesus Christ" (vv. 10-11, italics added).

The last point is the most sober of all. Jesus speaks of a division that is not merely for this life or for a few moments or years following death but for all eternity. It is the division between heaven and hell, joy and suffering, misery and the happiness of the Lord. In the last parable the sheep are separated from the goats, the latter going away "to eternal punishment, but the righteous to eternal life" (v. 46). In the other the faithful are invited to share their master's happiness (vv. 21, 23), but the wicked, lazy servant is thrown "outside, into the darkness, where there will be weeping and gnashing of teeth" (v. 30).

What a grim fate that is! *Darkness,* for it is apart from God, who is the source of all inner and outer light. *Outside,* because it is apart from Him who is the center of all things. In that outer darkness there is no hope, no joy, no love, no laughter. There is only weeping and the gnashing of teeth forever.

22

THE RICH MAN
AND LAZARUS

(Luke 16:19-31)

"There was a rich man who was dressed in purple and fine linen and lived in luxury every day. At his gate was laid a beggar named Lazarus, covered with sores and longing to eat what fell from the rich man's table. Even the dogs came and licked his sores.

"The time came when the beggar died and the angels carried him to Abraham's side. The rich man also died and was buried. In hell, where he was in torment, he looked up and saw Abraham far away, with Lazarus by his side. So he called to him, 'Father Abraham, have pity on me and send Lazarus to dip the tip of his finger in water and cool my tongue, because I am in agony in this fire.'

"But Abraham replied, 'Son, remember that in your lifetime you received your good things, while Lazarus received bad things, but now he is comforted here and you are in agony. And besides all this, between us and you a great chasm has been fixed, so that those who want to go from here to you cannot, nor can anyone cross over from there to us.'

"He answered, 'Then I beg you, father, send Lazarus to my father's house, for I have five brothers. Let him warn them, so that they will not also come to this place of torment.'

"Abraham replied, 'They have Moses and the Prophets; let them listen to them.'

" 'No, father Abraham,' he said, 'but if someone from the dead goes to them, they will repent.'

"He said to him, 'If they do not listen to Moses and the Prophets, they will not be convinced even if someone rises from the dead.' "

In all the Bible I do not believe there is a story more stirring or more disturbing than that of the rich man and Lazarus. It is stirring for its description of two men, one rich and one poor. They are set in contrast, and the contrast is not only between their circumstances in this life but also between their destinies in the life to come. The latter contrast is sharp, absolute, and permanent. The parable is disturbing because of its portrayal of the rich man's suffering. It is the only passage in the entire Bible that describes the actual thoughts, emotions, and words of somebody who is in hell. Hell itself is described elsewhere. There are warnings against it. But this is the only description of a person suffering in hell.

Besides the rather obvious contrasts we have between the rich man and the poor man in life, in death, and in their attitudes and knowledge following death, there are some additional but more subtle contrasts to be observed along the way.

THEIR EARTHLY CONDITION

The first contrast is an obvious one: the *rich man* "who was dressed in purple and fine linen and lived in luxury every day" and the *poor man,* Lazarus, who was "covered with sores and longing to eat what fell from the rich man's table" (Luke 16:19-21).

It is important to recognize that there is nothing here or elsewhere in the parable that condemns the rich man for being rich or praises the poor man for being poor. It is true that the rich man's riches undoubtedly worked to his hurt, for he apparently lived for those and nothing else. It *is* hard for the rich to enter heaven, as Jesus said elsewhere (Luke 18:25). It is also true that Lazarus's poverty worked to his spiritual good, for lacking earthly joys and comfort he undoubtedly turned his eyes to heaven and sought divine consolation. But regardless of those truths, it is still the case that nothing in the parable praises Lazarus for his poverty or condemns the rich man for his wealth. This is merely a description of two men: one rich, one poor. It is the way things were, and it is the way things are. There are always rich men, some of whom go to hell and some of whom go to heaven. There are always poor men, some of whom go to heaven and some of whom go to hell. But we are to focus on the spiritual distinction and not merely on the earthly one.

It is worth stressing that Lazarus's poverty was an indirect blessing to him, however, as I have indicated. We think of deprivation as irredeemably bad, but it obviously was not in his case. In his suffering Lazarus was forced to draw close to God, as the rich man was not. He must have filled his mind with the words of Scripture. He must have prayed. In that way he found God, and having found God he actually became richer than the rich man, though the world would never have been able to see that reality.

This leads to the most important thing that can be said about these two men in their earthly condition. We began with the superficial contrast: a rich man and a poor man. But at this point we need to elaborate. The man who was rich in this world's goods was actually poor spiritually, while the poor man was rich spiritually. From God's perspective this is a contrast between a *poor rich man* and a *rich poor man,* between one who did not have God although he had much else and one who had God although he lacked all else.

At that stage of their lives neither of those men would have willingly changed places with the other. The rich man did not value Lazarus's spiritual riches, so he would not have traded with him. And Lazarus, who valued the riches of a life with God, would not have traded with the rich man for his or anybody else's prosperity.

WHAT DEATH DID

The next stage in the story is the death of the two men: "The time came when the beggar died and the angels carried him to Abraham's side. The rich man also died and was buried" (v. 22). The rich man's burial must have been a fine thing. He had been favored in life, and some of the trappings of his earthly life must have followed him to the tomb. There would have been great pomp, great wealth, great heaps of flowers, great crowds of mourners. So far as Lazarus is concerned, it is not even said that he was buried, though he may well have been—unceremoniously, without pomp, unattended. But whether rich or poor, both died. In both cases, earthly life was terminated.

That is why death has been called "the great equalizer," though that is a misleading phrase in most cases. Brownlow North was a member of the English nobility who lived a carefree life until his conversion in 1854. After that he became a preacher and participated in the great awakenings in Ireland in 1859. North preached on this parable and tells at one point that many of the poor of his day had the idea that their condition in life would inevitably be righted in the next world.

One told him, "Sir, the thought that I shall die and have done with this life is my only happiness on earth. My one pleasure is to know that I must soon die, and that with my death my sorrows and my sufferings will be ended." Another said, "I have never known anything but misery; and now I am dying as I have lived. Do you think God will let me be miserable in the next world? It is the rich and not the poor who will suffer in the world to come."[1] Many have that view today, but it is as wrong today as it was then. Death is an equalizer only in the sense that all die: "golden lads and girls all must, as chimney-sweepers, come to dust" (Shakespeare). But it does not necessarily equal out the blessings and agonies of this world. On the contrary, it sometimes accentuates them.

That brings us to the third of the parable's contrasts, for according to this story the true riches of Lazarus were enhanced in the life to come, while the true poverty of the rich man was intensified. The rich man had lived without God in this world, so he died without God and had none of him in the life beyond. On the contrary, he had suffering. We are told that "in hell . . . he was in torment" (v. 23). Lazarus had lived with God here and had even more of Him in heaven. He was carried by the angels to Abraham's side. At that point we have a *poor rich man* growing *poorer* and a *rich poor man* growing *richer.* Not only did the rich man, who had no share in God, lose God—forever. He lost even those fine things (clothing, housing, and food) that he had had. Lazarus not only had God forever, he found other blessings besides.

That is what makes hell so terrible and heaven such a blessing. It

---

1. Brownlow North, *The Rich Man and Lazarus: A Practical Exposition of Luke 16:19-31* (Edinburgh and Carlisle, Pa.: Banner of Truth, 1979), pp. 17-23.

is not merely that hell is a place of suffering, though it is. It is that the loss of those in hell becomes ever more acute and the desperation of the lost ever more desperate. In heaven the pleasures of the saints increase forever.

THE MOMENTS AFTER DEATH

Up to now the contrast between the rich man and Lazarus has followed opposite but parallel lines: 1. earthly riches versus earthly poverty, 2. true poverty versus true riches, 3. an increase in true misery versus an increase in true blessing. But here the contrast varies. What happened to Lazarus and the rich man in the moments after death? Were they surprised, startled? Were their values in life challenged or reversed? The answer is that Lazarus's outlook remained essentially unchanged. He had known God in life, and God did not disappoint him afterward. If there was any difference in his experience, it was merely in the area of a growing awareness and appreciation of what he already had.

With the rich man it was quite different. Death for him was a shock, the rudest of all awakenings. It overthrew his value system entirely and introduced him to thoughts he never believed he would have. We may say of the poor rich man that he became *richer in knowledge* at the same time that he became *poorer in his spiritual state.*

He became richer in three areas. First, we are told that in hell "he looked up and saw Abraham far away, with Lazarus by his side" (v. 23). The rich man had never looked up to heaven in this life. If he even believed in heaven, it was with that kind of head knowledge that the devils have and do not profit by; and he may actually have doubted heaven's existence. He might have said, as many do today, "The only heaven that exists is the one I am able to make for myself here, and the only hell that exists is the hell some of us endure on earth." How that changed in the first moments after death! The rich man may have thought that dying was itself a hell, his only hell. But when he died he discovered that, far from being hell, even death was heaven compared to what he was now suffering. Lifting up his eyes he saw Lazarus and Abraham in heaven "far away."

I do not know whether our Lord means to teach here that those in hell can literally see those who are in heaven and that those in heaven can see those who are in hell. He may mean that. But again, it may be only figurative language. But what does it matter? If it is not a literal seeing with the eyes, it is at least a seeing with the understanding. And it means that in the moments following death, though the rich man may not have had any thoughts for heaven in this life, he now learned that there was a heaven as well as a hell and knew that he was not in heaven.

The second area in which that poor rich man became richer in knowledge was prayer. Not only did he come to know something that he did not know before—he did something that he had not done before. He began to pray, being convinced now that there was a reason to pray and something to pray for. He made many mistakes in prayer, as one would expect from a man who had not spent his life seeking and serving God. He prayed to Abraham instead of to God the Father. That was worthless, because only God answers prayer.

Again, he asked for the impossible: "Father Abraham, have pity on me and send Lazarus to dip the tip of his finger in water and cool my tongue, because I am in agony in this fire" (v. 24). When Abraham replied that this was not possible ("Between us and you a great chasm has been fixed, so that those who want to go from here to you cannot, nor can anyone cross over from there to us," v. 26), the rich man asked for another impossibility: "Then I beg you, father, send Lazarus to my father's house, for I have five brothers. Let him warn them, so that they will not also come to this place of torment" (v. 27). That also was useless ("If they do not listen to Moses and the Prophets, they will not be convinced even if someone rises from the dead," v. 31). Still, in spite of his errors about the only true object and nature of prayer, that was at least a genuine and heartfelt spiritual petition.

I do not mean to suggest that the rich man never did in life what we sometimes call praying, that is, "saying his prayers." He may well have. He was a Jew. He was probably an outstanding member of his community, and such people generally act religious. The rich man probably went to the synagogue and did what was expected of him. He would have recited prayers. But in all his life the rich man had not really prayed. No genuine, heart-rending, honest, God-seeking prayer had ever fallen from his lips. Yet now he was dead, and in the first moments after death he prayed. He prayed with more passion than he had ever shown for anything before.

The third thing the rich man learned is tragic: that his prayer was too late. In learning that he must have suffered the extremes of despair. I read an account of the despair of a family in which the mother died. She had been diagnosed as having cancer. She was to die in three months, but the family was unable to handle the prognosis. They could not believe that death was going to take their wife and mother and that there was nothing they could possibly do to change it. Helpless! That was the truly tragic element. But if that was the case in an instance of mere physical death, how much greater the feeling of helplessness and how acute the despair in the moments after death for those who are in hell and who learn that no amount of prayer is ever going to change their condition!

It is hard to imagine a tragedy greater than the one I am describing. To miss an opportunity is bad. To miss the greatest opportunity of all—the opportunity for life with God in heaven—is terrible. But to miss that forever and to know that you have missed it is a tragedy almost beyond endurance. Yet that is what Jesus said the rich man experienced. That was his fate.

In that we are introduced to one last contrast. There has been a contrast between the earthly conditions of the rich man and the beggar. There has been a contrast between their true state, the rich man actually being poor and the poor man actually being rich. There is a contrast between their experience in death; the poor rich man grew poorer, the rich poor man richer. There is a contrast between the natural unfolding of the poor man's experience and the abrupt awakening of the rich man to spiritual realities. In those quickly passing moments after death the rich man saw heaven, prayed in vain, and despaired. But there is this final contrast: between the *hopelessness* of the rich man's condition after death and the *hopefulness* of his condition before. After death there is no possibility of change. But in this life there is, and therefore we can rightly say "where there's life, there's hope," spiritually speaking.

This is the note on which I end: the opportunity that all who hear this parable still have, rather than on the end of opportunity that will come when death takes us. No matter who you are or what you may or may not have done, you are not yet in the position of the rich man who prayed but who, because he prayed in hell, prayed too late. For you it is not too late. You can pray; you can find God now. You can turn from sin and believe in the Lord Jesus Christ as your Savior. You can come to Christ in many ways, but it is only through Christ that you can come to heaven (John 14:6).

One of the great writers of the Elizabethan age was Christopher Marlowe, who wrote what is probably the classic treatment of the Faustus legend in English. Faustus was the character who, according to the story, sold his soul to the devil for secret knowledge and intense pleasure on earth. The devil gave him those things. But in the story there comes the moment when Faustus's earthly time runs out and the devil comes to take him away to damnation. In Marlowe's *Doctor Faustus,* Faustus, in despair, begs time to stop:

> O lente, lente, currite noctis equi!
> [The line means, "Run slowly, slowly, horses of the night!"]
> The stars move still, time runs, the clock will strike,
> The Devil will come, and Faustus must be damned.

Those words chill the heart. They paralyze the will. But praise to the God of all grace, those words are wrong. Why? Because it is not possible to sell your soul to the devil. The devil owns no one, and while we yet live it is not necessary that anyone be damned. Christ is preached. The door is open. Jesus Himself says, "Whosoever will may come."

Do not wait for signs. Do not wait for miracles. Abraham said that the brothers of the rich man would not believe "even if someone rises from the dead." You have the Scriptures, the Bible, and the story says, "They have Moses and the Prophets; let them listen to them" (v. 29). Listen to that word. Jesus said, "These are the Scriptures that testify about me" (John 5:39).

If you are not yet a believer in Jesus Christ, I commend that Word to you. I urge it on you for your soul's sake.

GENERAL INDEX

SCRIPTURE INDEX

Moody Press, a ministry of the Moody Bible Institute, is designed for education, evangelization, and edification. If we may assist you in knowing more about Christ and the Christian life, please write us without obligation: Moody Press, c/o MLM, Chicago, Illinois 60610.